Bob Whorton is a Methodist minist
in various Methodist circuits be
chaplain. His first chaplaincy pos
Rampton high-security psychiatri
four years he has been the chaplain at Sir Michael Sobell
House Hospice in Oxford. He has trained in counselling and
spiritual direction.

SPCK Library of Ministry

REFLECTIVE CARING

Imaginative listening to pastoral experience

SPCK Library of Ministry

BOB WHORTON

Sue

Love and peace

Bob

(SPCK) 1.3.11

First published in Great Britain in 2011

Society for Promoting Christian Knowledge
36 Causton Street
London SW1P 4ST
www.spckpublishing.co.uk

British Library Cataloguing-in-Publication Data
A catalogue record for this book is available from the British Library

ISBN 978–0–281–06413–7

1 3 5 7 9 10 8 6 4 2

Typeset by Graphicraft Ltd, Hong Kong
Printed in Great Britain by MPG Books Group

Produced on paper from sustainable forests

For Sue, my companion on the way

Contents

Preface

I'm not sure I could have written this book without the encouragement of the pastoral team at Sir Michael Sobell House Hospice, Oxford. With the help of Beryl Hill, a specialist community nurse, I set up this team of skilled volunteers in 2008–9. The volunteers (who come from different spiritual backgrounds) work mainly on the ward in the hospice, listening to and accompanying the patients and families who come to us. Every month they attend a two-hour group supervision meeting where they reflect on their encounters.

I wrote this book first of all for the pastoral team. Through the writing I wanted to describe my own practice of reflection and see if it might be of use to other people. I would hammer out a chapter and then email it to everyone. They gave feedback on the text, tried out some of the exercises (see the Appendix) and told me the project was worthwhile when I was faltering. I am grateful to the team for believing in this writing.

I want to thank my wife Sue Whorton, my son Phil Whorton and Raymond Avent for reading the manuscript and giving me their helpful responses. Thank you also to Stanton House Retreat Centre, in Stanton St John, just outside Oxford, where many of the chapters emerged in draft form and whose staff gave me their hospitality. I am grateful to those who have listened to me over the years, and to Isabel Gregory for accompanying me on my soul journey these last two years; those who work with us at the soul level influence us profoundly, and in the following pages you will sometimes hear echoes of Isabel's voice. I am also grateful to my supervisors, who have helped me to reflect honestly on my work in the hospice.

And thank you to my chaplaincy colleagues, past and present, who have shared the adventure of service with me.

Finally I want to express my appreciation of the patients, families and staff (paid and unpaid) at Sobell House, for this book has grown out of my relationship with this very special place.

Introduction

I wake up on a workday feeling low and defeated. Taking
my tea into the garden I am remembering fragments
of dreams. I sit down without enthusiasm in the sun-
shine of a new day. As I allow myself to sink down into
my mood it is the voice of my anxious child-self that
I hear. 'How am I going to . . . ? I shouldn't have . . . I've
got to . . . It all feels too much . . . I want to run away . . .'.
I try simply to hear his voice. This is difficult because
there is another part of me wanting to tell him to be
quiet and get a grip. Then I put my arms around my
child-self; I thank him for being able to speak to me.
And I hold him in a love that is greater than me.

Reflective practice is 'in'. Those who work as volunteers
or professionals in any helping or listening work today are
expected to reflect on what they are doing. In this way we
are to improve our competency and skill levels in the work
we do. But how do we actually do it? Sally and Paul Nash,
in their helpful book, *Tools for Reflective Ministry*,[1] outline
the reflective frameworks and models most commonly used
in a variety of settings today. When we have different choices
to make about how we use our time, we tend to do those
things we enjoy doing. This book outlines a simple reflective
process using imaginative techniques that, while inevitably
stretching at times, can be *enjoyable*.

Let me tell you at the outset that in this book I have some
imaginative conversations with Jesus . . . and I use passages
from the Bible to reflect with. You might think that is fine,
or it might sound odd. If it sounds strange, let me assure
you that this book is about *soul* – and I believe that each of

us has awareness of our soul. If you are not from the Christian tradition, or find you are uncomfortable with using Christian texts, I encourage you to find corresponding passages in other sacred writings or in secular literature.

I would like to tell you a little about myself. When I was 17 I had a mystical experience. As a result I desired to serve God and my fellow human beings. At first I thought I should become a social worker, but then I started leading services in Methodist churches and eventually offered myself for ministry in the Methodist Church. I knew that serving God and people would not be easy, but I had no real idea about what I had let myself in for. In particular I did not realize it would mean the joy and suffering involved in travelling to the depths of who I am as a human being. For the last 28 years I have been in full-time ministry in a variety of church and chaplaincy settings. Currently I am a chaplain at Sir Michael Sobell House Hospice in Oxford.

I have always been interested in what happens between two people when one of them sets out to listen to the other. It sounds so simple, doesn't it? But without self-awareness we can be at best ineffectual and at worst actively harmful to others. I have come to realize how important it is for me to reflect as honestly as I can on the reactions I have in my work. By giving attention to these I am better equipped to be with another person in a listening relationship. If we are not able to work with the distress inside us, which is a mixture of our own pain and the pain of others, then one of two things is likely to happen. Either we subtly blame the person in need for adding to the burden of our pain or we (unconsciously) ask them to make *us* feel better in the face of *their* pain. The reflective process is therefore a necessary one. We need to reflect by ourselves but, in addition, we are greatly helped by individual or group supervision.

The phrase I use for the process I describe is *soul reflection*. We often use the words *soul* and *spirit* to mean the same thing.

In the National Health Service (NHS) the task of hospital chaplains is described as 'caring for the spirit'.[2] Spiritual care in a hospital setting today means supporting someone as they address the big questions of meaning, identity, connection and belief. In my own work I have – admittedly quite recently – become much more comfortable with the language of *soul*. Soul is grounded, personal, everyday and here-and-now; it is the part of my being that experiences the divine in me. By contrast, spirit refers to the heights of divine love, absolutes and universal truths; if we are not careful, spirit can leap up and away into the upper atmosphere. Soul reflection is the process of paying attention, without judgement, to inner reactions that bubble up from the different selves inside us. When we listen to a person who is experiencing challenges, there will be all sorts of responses in our soul. We will find ourselves in contact with our disorganized, confusing inner world – this contains our personal history, wounds, emotional and thinking responses, and is uniquely ours. It is like a lump of unshaped clay that has the potential to become a rather nice vase; this is what we are invited to give our attention to.

This inner world needs hospitality. The words hospice, hospital and hospitality come from the Indo-European root *ghosti*. From this root we get our words 'guest', 'host' and 'hostile'. I am used to playing the host at our hospice; it is one of the pieces of my work that I like best. I may welcome people when they first arrive, expressing the hope that it will be a good place for them. And at times I will 'scoop up' a distressed person at the reception desk and give them a cup of tea. I wish the stranger to feel like an honoured guest. But there are parts of my own self that are strangers and need my hospitality. Some of them feel dangerous – hostile even. These are the parts of my being that are normally hidden safely from public view. If they cannot get my attention through a whisper, then at some point they will do so with a scream. These also need my welcome. If I am to be able to offer hospitality to people in the hospice and listen to them, I need to learn how to welcome the various components of my own self as esteemed guests.[3]

Let me now address some possible criticisms of this book. The first comes from part of my own self. He accuses me of going on a self-glorifying power trip: 'You just want people to tell you how wonderful you are for writing such a self-revealing book', he mocks (as you will discover, I use my own reactions and imaginative journeys as the bones of the writing). The problem is that I know he is right. But I also know it is not the whole truth. By writing in the way I do, I want to model something. I want to say to you, 'This is how I've tried doing it, now you go and play with your reactions in the way that is right for you.' The gift of wholeness is never for ourselves alone (see the story of the Rainmaker in Chapter 15).

One of the criticisms of counselling, spiritual accompaniment and pastoral care is that this kind of work does not affect the political realities of the world we live in. By our caring we may be teaching people to adjust better to unjust or at best amoral social situations. I feel the weight of this argument, but change has to start somewhere. Soul reflection is a way of transformation – if we are becoming more whole, and the people we are listening to are becoming a bit more whole, then in a small but significant way society is becoming more whole.

Another criticism of this kind of reflective work is: 'Can't we just have a conversation with someone without analysing what's going on all the time?' Of course we can. But those of us who want to listen to and care for others can learn to do it better. By reflecting creatively on our work we become more aware, and that awareness brings a new freedom and spaciousness into the caring relationship that is helpful to the person we are listening to.

I also realize that not everyone reading this book will be involved in the work of hospice and palliative care. But my hope is that you will easily be able to transfer the ideas in this book across into your working situation. And finally I want to assure you that I *do* have good days at work! Reading these chapters may give the impression that my inner world is so full of complex, difficult reactions that I am in a state of perpetual misery. This is not the case. It is in the nature of a book like this that areas of difficulty and challenge are the ones highlighted.

Part 1 of the book sets the scene by showing how our different selves reveal themselves to us through our imagination, and here I underline the importance of a playful approach to reflection. A listening relationship in which the depths of human experience are explored calls for a reflective process that can hold both parties. Part 2 details some soul reactions – together with my reflections on them – that arise as a result of caring for those in need. For those of you who wish to have some starting points for your own soul reflections, I have added an Appendix containing suggestions for reflective work based on each chapter.

In the following pages I sometimes refer to encounters with patients, and in order to preserve confidentiality I have changed names and significant details. There are two exceptions to this: Jamie Paterson's family have kindly allowed me to use the address for Jamie's funeral at the end of Chapter 2; and for the section headed 'Direct or indirect' in Chapter 3, Paula Gray kindly gave me permission to write about the meeting I describe there.

Part 1

A WAY OF REFLECTING

1

Many selves

Our garden in Oxford has many inhabitants: an apple tree dropping its fruit because of the dry weather; a squirrel that likes to skip along the fence; herbs growing in the little garden I made out of old concrete blocks; an old cherry tree that no longer produces leaves; a pair of goldfinches who love to search for insects in this tree; a visiting rat; flowers in the border; fish in the pond; bamboo rustling in the wind. Each of the inhabitants has its own character, and together they make the whole. So with you and I. We are one person, but we contain many different selves.

In 1410 Andrei Rublev painted his icon of the Trinity. We have a copy of it in the hospice chapel. It shows the three mysterious visitors who came to Abraham and Sarah (Gen. 18.1–15). Abraham offered them hospitality under the Oak of Mamre, and at the end of the feast he was told that his wife Sarah would give birth to a child in her old age. Rublev depicts the strangers as the three persons of the Trinity. When I look at the icon I see balance and energy. Love seems to flow through the characters and between them, so that they are never still, always held in each other's embrace. It has been pointed out that the three figures can be contained within one circle.

The Judaeo-Christian tradition asserts that we are made in God's image. If this is so, then perhaps each human being is called to become like the Holy Trinity. Our many selves are meant to flow in and out of each other, delighting in each other's energy. All of these selves belong to the greater self, and love seeks to make pathways between them, ultimately bringing about integration. When this happens we can be truly attentive to people around us – because we have welcomed our many selves we can go on to welcome the many selves in the person we are attempting to listen to.

Except that we know this is a work in progress. We know that the rat *and* the goldfinch will keep appearing in the garden of our soul. The task is to keep on offering hospitality to both.

Welcoming the wounded self

If someone asks me the simple question, 'How are you today, Bob?' I am sometimes not sure how to respond. It may be that I am closed down so that I am only dimly aware of my inner world, or it may be that there are so many things going on inside me that I cannot speak clearly about them. The different parts of myself may be saying different things. I may feel anxious, irritated, tired and hopeful all at once! My daily moods, states of mind and reactions to people around me are complex. And they have their origin in these many selves that make up 'me'.

Some of the selves I know only too well. They are very loud. For example, there is a part of me that will shout, 'You've got it wrong again!' at the least provocation. Some have been silenced because I am ashamed of what they tell me. Some are damaged, and need extra love and care. And some have a gentle voice that I only hear by listening very carefully ('You are the beloved'). I need to pay particular attention to the quiet whispers of the emergent self; this is the self whom I do not yet fully trust but who is beckoning me towards wholeness. He tells me of my goodness, speaks in my dreams and invites me to trust myself more; he also challenges my assumptions and threatens to turn my world upside down.

The wounded, shameful selves are very important to me because they will be particularly vocal when I am present to another wounded, vulnerable human being (there is particular power when a wounded part of ourselves meets a similar wound in the other person). I may find that a part of me is fearful or sexually aroused; I could feel helpless, exhausted or full of despair. I need to learn how to offer these selves my particular hospitality. The ego does not want the damaged, shadow parts of myself to exist; he would expel them into the outer darkness if he could, so that 'I' could be pure and free and good. However, my experience has been that the consequences of such attempted expulsion are dire in the extreme: the rejected self comes back and bites me on the bum – with the jaws of a dragon. The dynamic of repression reads like this: 'I am ashamed of this part of me. I will push it away. Thank God it's gone.' But it has not gone. It goes deep down into the unconscious and will re-emerge at another time with a powerful destructive energy. The much more difficult and courageous path is the one of allowing the damaged selves to speak to me. The dynamic here is: 'OK, this is me. I may not like it, but this is part of my God-given shape at this time. I will intentionally put my arms around this self.' And it may just be that instead of a monster, I discover a little child who feels hurt and abandoned.

In the hospice, some staff bring medication to patients, some bring creative or complementary therapies and some bring food and drink. But as a pastoral carer the only thing I bring is myself. This being myself, in this moment of time, is all I have to offer. So the more I am aware of the different selves within me – their voices, tricks and energies – the more I will be able to simply *be* with the other person. If my different selves know that they are heard and loved within the community of the self, they will allow me to do this; I can try to give my whole attention to the other person. A child who knows that they are loved is likely to be quiet and well-mannered at dinner-time when guests are present. A child who rarely gets any parental attention is likely to throw their food around. When I find one of my inner selves starting to throw food around, I cannot listen properly; I will not be fully present to the other person, because part of me will be listening to this unruly self and trying to contain him. This angry or grieving or helpless part of me is not 'bad'; he just needs to be welcomed home.

The banquet

How are we to offer this hospitality to our different selves? I recall an imaginative exercise based on the parable of the Great Banquet (Luke 14.15–24). In this story a man plans a banquet for his friends. They send excuses and decline to come, so the man invites the poor of the town to the feast and, when there is still room, the homeless wanderers in the countryside.

In the first part of the exercise I list the different parts of the self and the roles I have, with a brief description of each (or I might draw them). Then I imagine a magnificent banqueting hall containing the finest food and drink. The hall has an anteroom, and one by one I imagine my different selves coming into this room, being greeted – by Christ or another figure – and invited into the hall itself. It is important to be playful and to allow actions and conversations to happen naturally; I need to let the ideas come without analysing them or judging them. The dominant parts of the self may well appear first, but I can allow the others to wander shyly into the anteroom in their own time.

I last did this exercise while at a retreat house, sitting next to a stream and observing a group of ducks. Intriguingly there were the same number of ducks as the number of selves I had noted down. These ducks had amazing energy. They were feeding, fighting, cleaning themselves, bobbing underwater, waddling up the lawn, waddling back, climbing up the rocky ledge – such a variety of movements and interactions. Here was a community of ducks mirroring the complex reactions within myself in the community that is me.

In the exercise, I encountered to my surprise a beautiful lady who related to each of my selves with great courtesy and warmth. My child-self was scared of meeting people and did not want to go into the hall. She gently persuaded him, and they went in to play with a table covered with Lego®; together they built a large bridge, and in my imagination the bridge was from fear on one side to love on the other. The ascetic walked into the hall as an old man with a stick. He is the part of me who tries very hard to be holy. He gravely took a seat and asked the lady for a little bread and water. 'But the King is here,' she said, 'this is a time for feasting.' He replied, 'Thank you, but I will shame you all with my great self-sacrifice. It will give me great pleasure.' The wounded one did not want to go in, fearing judgement and rejection; he was received with an expansive gentleness and love. And the contemplative found himself in a beautiful, moving circle of light; as he was held in this place, he found he could invite others to share in it. There was a different 'feel' with each of the selves. Some of them were deadly familiar, and I could laugh at them; others were crying out for compassion; still others seemed quite new, in need of a little more elbow room in the community.

We do not need to be ruled by the old selves who command operations from their comfortable armchairs by the fire. Newer selves can come along with their camp-chairs, warm themselves and watch the expressions on the faces of the old commanders as they gently but firmly make plans for the future operations of the community. I have found life, humour and great energy in playing with the banquet exercise.

The room

I was given an exercise once while I was on a retreat, and I have developed it a little. It is another way of welcoming our different selves. I imagine myself descending a spiral staircase. This helps me to descend quite quickly inside myself. At the bottom is a hallway and a door. In my pocket is a key, and I find that the key fits the lock and I can go in. This is my room. I furnish it as I wish. The room may change a little on each visit but I always find there is a window looking out on to the sea. After exploring the room and making myself at home again, I make myself a cup of coffee. I sit down and feel a deep peace entering me. After a while there is a gentle knocking at the door. I get up, open the door and there is the Christ (or a wise person). I invite him in and give him a cup of coffee. We talk honestly to each other. I tell him about the parts of myself that are most troublesome at the moment. He listens, responds and loves me. When the conversation comes to an end I show him out, then leave also. I lock the door and ascend the spiral staircase, taking back with me a little fragment of peace.

Reflecting in the listening relationship

The only way I can identify the needs of my different selves is by attending to the various reactions I experience in my inner being. As I listen to another person and react inwardly, I may have some clues as to what is going on in that moment of listening. But I also need to give myself time to reflect later on. I freely admit I do not always do this – life moves on quickly. Yet if I do not allow myself the space for reflection on something important, my needy selves will start throwing food around again. The reflective practice I use is a very simple, intuitive one: I notice reactions inside myself; I try not to ignore them or judge them; I play with these reactions in a variety of ways so that I learn something from them; very gradually I notice something changing in my work.

'Play' is the key word here. The art of reflection can be very enjoyable so long as we don't take ourselves too seriously. Of course there will be times of pain when we are faced with a wounded part of ourselves that needs much attention and love, but equally there will be times when we are delighted with what we are discovering. Journaling, writing dialogues with the parts of the self we scarcely know, drawing and painting, dancing to music in the privacy of our front room, writing spontaneous poetry, hammering out a compelling tune on a keyboard, letting our dreams speak to us – these are some of the ways we can play with the material. Through this process I discover more about what lies behind my fear, my sadness, my anger or my tiredness, and I find I can slowly move into a different sort of space. I cannot *make* this happen; it is a question of trusting the process. The new space is less cluttered, so there is less to trip over and it feels very different. There is much less anxiety and pressure. I do not have to *do* much at all. And of course I need endless patience with myself because I go backwards as well as forwards in the work.

I have come to the conclusion that it is foolish for me to believe I can make sense of my different selves and attend to my inner reactions completely by myself. My ego does not like this conclusion. He wants to do it all by himself and not suffer the humiliation of the less 'worthy' selves parading themselves in public. Supervision, psychotherapy, spiritual accompaniment and the less formal conversations with colleagues and members of my family have all helped me to begin loving my different selves instead of trying to kill them off. I am slowly discovering a more spacious self.

But still a critical voice tells me that this work of soul reflection is merely self-indulgence – the narcissistic spirit of the age masquerading as reflective practice. Let me talk with this voice (Critical Voice – c):

c   It's self-indulgent, isn't it?

b   I'm not sure.

c   You know it's true. You're only interested in yourself at the end of the day.

b   I'm really curious about my own reactions and I do want more wholeness . . .

c   I told you so.

b   But I also know – I really know – that unless I can accept the strangers in me, the shadow selves that I don't want to acknowledge, then it will be impossible for me to accept a skeletal old woman with a revolting fungating cancer, or someone from a totally different culture . . .

c   I'm not sure I believe you.

b   I suppose the bottom line is whether the reflective work takes you away from other people and inside yourself, or if it frees you up to reach out better to those around you.

2

Imagination

Rich resources of the imagination are available to us in our work of listening to others. Imagination is the language of soul, and through it we can converse with our different selves. Pictures, conversations and dreams can bubble up, which enable connection between the outer self and the inner world. In medieval times it was understood that there were different ways of knowing things. A distinction was made between *ratio* and *intellectus*. *Ratio* is the power of logical thought; it is about examining, defining and categorizing. *Intellectus* is more difficult to describe; it is a knowledge that is not grasped but given, and it is more akin to intuition – insights and inspiration flow through the creative imagination. When we take imagination seriously we open ourselves to knowing things in a different way. *Ratio* says to me, 'Don't trust these inner dialogues and imaginings; you're just making them up to make yourself feel better – they're flights of fancy.' But *intellectus* replies, 'Trust the fruits; if this process leads to more openness, love, acceptance and wholeness, then you can't be far wrong.' We need both of course – the tough questioning *ratio* brings and the grace-filled inspiration of *intellectus*.

Labyrinth

A labyrinth is a pathway that is walked in an intentional way, and many experience a connection with their inner being as they walk it. It is different from a maze. If you walk into a maze you can get lost or come up against a dead end, whereas the path of a labyrinth takes you round and round into its centre and then out again (although it is possible to become disorientated). Labyrinths have been discovered all over the world, some thousands of years old. Perhaps the most famous is to be found in Chartres Cathedral, built for pilgrims who could no longer travel to the Holy Land because of the Crusades – they would come to Chartres and walk the labyrinth instead.

Labyrinths are being made in many different places today – including hospices. You can walk the labyrinth how you want to (equally, you can dance, skip or run round it – or be pushed in a wheelchair). It is a form of spiritual play in which the outer and inner journey become entwined. Pause as you enter, perhaps briefly giving thanks, then walk round the pathway to the centre, asking for help in letting something go inside you. When you arrive at the centre it is a time to be still, to receive something; often people experience peace here. And then you follow the same pathway out, taking the gift with you. Sometimes people take a question with them into the labyrinth; once I took in the question, 'How am I to live?' As I walked out the answer formed in my heart: 'As a child of wonder.' People of faith or of no faith can walk the labyrinth, and many are bowled over by what they experience.

Lizzie Hopthrow, the chaplain at Pilgrims Hospice in Canterbury (soon to retire), has made the labyrinth available to patients, families and staff in the hospice. She began by making hand-held labyrinths in the day hospice that could be traced with the finger, and the patients then wanted to make one they could walk. Today there is a beautiful labyrinth in the grounds;[1] many who have walked it have found emotional release and a powerful connection with their soul journey.

The labyrinth, with its many layers of meaning, allows us to reflect from the soul, and it 'works' through the imagination.

I have found all sorts of striking images in it: wholeness; putting one foot in front of the other and seeing what happens; the cross (if you draw a labyrinth you start by making a cross shape); getting lost and finding your way; being held in love; a womb at the centre. The delightful thing is that each person will find their own images. We can walk into the labyrinth bringing our listening work with us – a person we are concerned about or a conversation that did not go so well – and see what bubbles up inside us.

Wood for the shoulders

I want now to look at some powerful images that have come to my assistance in the last few years. Having worked for some time in the hospice, I lived through a time of feeling profoundly useless. I was not sure that anything I was doing had any meaning or that I was being helpful to patients and their families. I was tired and fearful that I would not be able to continue in the work. I did not want to move on but I was aware that my resources were much depleted.

During this time I found it very helpful to simply read through the Passion narrative, noting the slight differences in the Gospels. This narrative includes the whole build-up to the crucifixion, and the word passion means 'being acted upon' (hence 'passive'). In the text I discovered a man facing his own uselessness. The Gospel writers make it sound as though Christ is still in control, that everything is planned and that it is all happening as the Scriptures have foretold. But there are times when another picture breaks through. The prayer in Gethsemane is desperate. Jesus is wondering if he has got it all wrong, and he really does not want to face his own dying with this sense of failing in his mission. On the cross he cries out from the depths of his soul while he is dying. It is a cry of hopelessness and abandonment. He is dying in failure. He has not managed to get his message through to the people, apart from a very few. They have gladly received the bread and fishes, and the healing that he has brought to their broken bodies; but these were the same people who later spat on him and gladly handed him over to torture and the slow death of crucifixion. What has it all been for?

Images work at very profound levels. They literally *work* for us, on our behalf, making a home for themselves in the unconscious where they do their healing work. I found a very containing and helpful image in the narrative:

> After they had mocked him, they took off the robe and put his own clothes on him. Then they led him away to crucify him. As they were going out, they met a man from Cyrene, named Simon, and they forced him to carry the cross.
>
> (Matt. 27.32–34)

Cyrene is in Libya, and Simon is often depicted as the first African Christian. He is reported by Mark to be the father of Rufus and Alexander, who were obviously well known in the early Christian community. However, it is likely that Simon was a Jew living in the established Jewish community in Cyrene. This group had their own synagogue in Jerusalem, and so it is not surprising to find Simon travelling to celebrate the Passover in Jerusalem.

In my imagination I sense his dismay, revulsion and fear when he is compelled by the Roman soldiers to carry the horizontal crosspiece for an execution. He had come to worship and take some holiday, and instead found himself taking part in a crucifixion. I pondered my own sense of call. Early on I thought I had been called to heroic ministry, doing great and exciting things for God. But in each ministry setting I have found myself sooner or later carrying a cross.

I thought myself into the scene, taking the cross onto my shoulders, and I found the image surprisingly comforting. I felt the wood on my shoulders. It was strangely warm and had the right fit. I found I could 'carry it around' with me during the day. The wood was there, resting on my shoulders, as I lived out my day in the hospice.

How did this image *work* for me? It was one that fitted exactly my experience at that time. My helplessness matched Christ's helplessness and therefore I was no longer alone. In some way I felt we were carrying the cross together, and there was great consolation in that experience.

Dry bones

The following is part of the record of a structured imaginative exercise where the images of Ezekiel 37 became very meaningful to me. In this passage the prophet is despairing because of the collapse of the nation of Israel; he sees the people as a valley of dry bones, in desperate need of God's revitalizing breath. I find I need a clear, containing structure for an exercise when I am struggling within. The dry bones of the passage became a powerful symbol for the dryness of my inner life, and there was a clear movement from disconnection to connection. I prayed by tapping away at my keyboard in my office at the hospice:

I make the sign of the cross.
I remember that God is here at this moment of my history.
He is acquainted with all my ways.
He is present to me in this particular experience when my spirit is dull and unresponsive.
I think of an image for myself at this moment: a broken cup that cannot contain anything.
My feelings: weary; dull; flat; sad; don't belong; disconnected; self-pitying; meaningless; everything an effort; guilty that I'm doing this exercise and not something useful.

15

What is the gift I pray for? I want to live and to be a
transmitter of God's life.

Method: to use Ezekiel's vision of the dry bones and
apply it to my current situation.

I then allowed different sets of my 'bones' to speak truthfully
about the disconnection they experienced. The first belonged
to my inner child, the second belonged to the wounded self
and the third to the adventurer. I simply allowed my imagination to speak, and this proved very cathartic. I then asked God
to send his Spirit into these bones in turn. I imagined God
speaking to the different selves. This was very real, liberating
and joyful. The bones came to life.

And to complete the prayer, a patient being pushed in
a wheelchair by his wife stops in the corridor outside
the office. I kneel by him and we talk. We look into
each other's eyes. There is connection. I promise to
make sure he gets to the day centre tomorrow.

Thanksgiving:

Thank you for life beginning to flow like a stream of
water across the sand.

Thank you for people beyond my self.

Thank you for Sobell House and its special gift of
hospitality.

Thank you for the breath of life.

At the beginning I was guilty about spending time on my inner
life. But the encounter with the patient at the end shows the
fruit of this sort of prayer. The imaginative exercise freed me
up to serve again.

A new bicycle

A member of staff was very upset by something that had
happened. I offered to listen but he did not wish me to.

The rational part of my mind accepted this, but in my soul I experienced a profound sense of rejection. We have a choice when something like this happens: we can grit our teeth, push the feelings away and get on with our work (as this member of staff had decided to do); or we can risk offering hospitality to the powerful reaction. One technique is to 'lower ourselves down' deliberately into the feeling, holding on as best we can to an awareness that we are loved.

I decided I needed to do something about my reaction in order to be at all useful for the rest of the day, so I sat down at the computer and went deeper into the experience of rejection. What was this feeling like? I imagined a deep well and typed away as the images came along (the typing helped to ground me).

> The well has slimy green walls. I go down to the bottom of it. Here is a discarded shopping trolley and a broken bicycle, lying in dirty water. I know I'm encountering the part of me that feels discarded, uncared for and unrecognized. I notice that my breathing is tight; I feel very tired. I invite Christ into the scene. He takes the bicycle and starts to repair it. He fits new pedals and a new chain, straightens the wheels and polishes up the chrome. Then he puts new inner tubes into new tyres. And it's all done with great gentleness and care. I hear the words, 'I love you with an everlasting love.' The repair of the bicycle feels very good. It's not perfect and it still needs a respray, but it's back together again.

At the end of this imaginative exercise I was calm. I felt loved and able to continue with the day. We need to trust that images will come to us when we need them. I cycle to work each day, and for me the bicycle is a beautiful symbol of movement. The images that work for us may well be those that connect to our everyday lives. I also acknowledge that the above is 'imaginative first-aid'. The unrecognized parts of myself at the bottom of the well need much more loving attention, but at least I discovered they were there!

Dreams

Dreams can tell us things we need to know but do not want to know. Here is a good example of the unconscious telling me something important:

> Something is alive under the water; I wonder if it really can be alive. Whatever it is, it needs my help. I'm terrified of what I may find if I reach down into the water, but I take my courage in my hands and do it. I see a circular shape – I haul out a young woman and then a dog who resolves into Tess (one of our dogs). The girl seems fine. I hold Tess and she pants in my arms, recovering her breath. The girl says to me, 'Four minutes longer and we would have died.' I'm amazed they could survive for so long under the water.

I understand this dream as an invitation to more wholeness. The young woman represents my anima or soul, and Tess my animal, physical being. I've been keeping them under water because of fear, but when they emerge they are not frightening at all. There is a sense of urgency in the 'four minutes': time is running out for me to see what I need to see. The circular shape is the whole person I am called to become.

It can be useful to 'talk' to our dream figures – by having a conversation with them we can find out more about what they wish to reveal to us. This can be done through writing or by imagining the figure seated in a chair next to us and vocalizing our thoughts. Sometimes it can take time for the meaning of dreams to dawn upon us; it was only when, after several months, I went back to the dream I describe that I *saw* what it was imaging for me. Of course, some dreams do not come with such readily available explanations!

The cries of the inner child

The everyday pressures of the hospice are huge, for it acts as a container for human anguish, loss, despair, helplessness and confusion. Those of us who work there get used to being in this environment, but every now and then the container does not feel so safe. When I am feeling vulnerable my child-self is not far away. He can become very anxious and afraid in the face of powerful emotion, and will need my attention. These reactions feel very early (developmentally), and so the imaginative response needs to correspond to this early experience. I sometimes find it helpful to imagine myself as a baby or young child; I allow myself to be cradled and rocked in a comfortable rocking chair in the arms of the divine feminine, or I will feed at her breast. Even a short period of reflecting in this way can restore my inner balance. The message I hear is, 'You are OK. You are held in a greater love.' I then feel much safer as I reach out to others with the gift of myself.

Crossing the water

Sometimes we can invite others to join us in imaginative 'play'. Jamie was a young man with a double challenge. He had been living with schizophrenia since his teens and now, in his late twenties, had a cancer that would inevitably lead to his death. I enjoyed my visits with Jamie in the hospice. He was interested in everyone and asked me about why I had become a minister and what sort of training I had had. His family were wonderful with him. One day I went into his room and saw a card pinned to his noticeboard. This became the starting point for an imaginative journey. When Jamie died unexpectedly at home a few weeks later, the family asked me to conduct his funeral service. This was my tribute to Jamie:

We only met a handful of times
But I'm glad our lives touched.
I saw you as a man on a mission
Needing to know Stuff –
Such a lot of curiosity.
We went to the hospice library one day
You and me, up the difficult stairs
With Anna the physio,
Both of us loving her beautiful energy.
We went because you needed to know Stuff
About disease and dying.

I was in playful mood one day:
'Would you like to try an imaginative exercise?' I asked.
You were willing to play.
I took the card from the board.
I saw a landing stage on the edge of a lake (you saw
    a river),
The water so still, mountains across the other side.
You thought a boat would be a good idea
So you climbed aboard,
And as you got to the other side
Another experience of the feminine –
One of our cleaners wandered in and started mopping
    under the bed.
You got out of the boat and I thought you might like
    to meet a wise person!
You met.
'What do you want to talk about?' I asked.
You thought carefully.
'Probably we'd talk about the geology of the mountains.'
I take this in.
'Would you want to talk about yourself at all?' I ask.
'I'd probably talk about having a terminal illness and
    dying,' you say.

I wonder whether to ask you more about this, but decide
   against it.
The menu for tomorrow's food is delivered.
And you get in the boat and return to this side again.
This side,
But not to stay for long.
Because you got in the boat again
Without our wishing it or planning it,
To make the journey you needed to make
Into love and light and freedom and goodness.

Crossing water is symbolic of dying and new life. In Greek
mythology the ferryman Charon carries people across the
River Styx, from the land of the living to the land of the
dead. The Israelites crossed the River Jordan at the end of
their journey from Egypt into the freedom of the Promised
Land. Crossing the Jordan has become a metaphor for dying
and entering into heaven. It is interesting to note that when
Jesus crosses the Sea of Galilee in the Gospels, something
new is about to happen. A storm will be calmed, hungry
people will be fed, a madman will find sanity and be clothed
in love . . .

By using the image of crossing the water with Jamie, I was
inviting him to consider his death in a symbolic and hope-
fully non-threatening way. And by introducing a 'wise person'
to him, I was suggesting that there were resources he could
access on this journey. I was aware of the risk I was taking
in attempting an inner journey with someone who had a
psychiatric illness, but I kept the visualization light and matter of fact. There were two 'interruptions' – someone deli-
vering the food menu, and the cleaner – but these actually
helped, keeping us both firmly anchored in the room.

Imagination takes us from the outer to the inner world,
and I have been surprised by the power of some of the
images that have come to my aid as I have reflected on my

work. There is a strong sense of gift here – the gift of *intellectus*. If I try to make the images come they will run away. They come to me in my need – a refreshment for the soul, like a cup of tea on a hot day. And they tell me what is really going on.

The NHS work-culture today desperately needs the resources of imagination. A cold, bureaucratic, target-driven approach leaves us at best uninspired and at worst resistant and angry. We need to harness in the workplace the kind of imagination and play that go into Comic Relief and Children in Need events. The energy that goes into dressing up and acting silly for a day is the sort of energy we need in reflection. To engage seriously with the question, 'What is going on inside me as I try to care for another?' takes energy and courage, and those who try to care for others need the gifts of imagination day in, day out. Imagination and a playful, reflective approach quite simply enable us to continue doing the work we do.

3

Play

A playful attitude

Let us go out to play. Sir Michael Sobell House is an NHS hospice, and we rely on the NHS for approximately two-thirds of our funding. It's good that we are able to benefit from this level of funding; not so good that what happens in the rest of the Oxford Radcliffe Hospitals Trust affects us also. The Trust Board needs to get rid of the debt that has built up over the years, and today's mantra is 'Do more with less.' There is fear in the air: fear of not meeting the targets, fear of change, fear of redundancies, and close behind the fear is anger – 'How can they do this to us?' Fear swoops down upon the workforce and then flies up again to the senior managers, taking the anger with it. The managers then become more fearful and angry, and so the negative cycle continues. Fear and anger mean that people do not always think straight; the solution grasped is the first that seems to make sense. Playfulness does not do well in a bureaucratic, rational, professionalized culture – and it does not do well in the face of fear and anger. Yet a playful attitude is exactly what is needed when there is a crisis brewing. Play is at the heart of reflection, and the 'virtuous' cycle of reflection counteracts the negative one. It helps us stand back from and to one side of the difficulties – out of the firing line for a moment. Then it becomes possible to play with what is going on; to play with outrageous, crazy solutions that have not been thought up before; to play around with a vision for the

23

future. In this way what is *really* going on can be discovered, perhaps for the first time, and different ways of proceeding can be assessed.

In an environment of scarce resources, employees have to prove their worth – chaplains included: they have to demonstrate that what they do makes a difference. So there is a pressure on chaplains to do research and provide evidence for the effectiveness of their practice. Most have to submit returns to management each month detailing their activity: how many visits, how many communions, how much staff support, how many teaching slots and so on. I do understand this. We have to demonstrate that what we do is worthwhile and of benefit to the organizations we work for. But it can paralyse us too and squeeze the playful attitude out of us.

And play is serious business. Think of a child. Through play a child learns how to solve problems ('How do I get the cat to eat my rattle?'). Through play a child discovers a larger world ('This snow tastes really good'). Through playing with others a child learns about relationships ('For some reason she doesn't like me biting her leg'). Play enables all sorts of amazing developments to occur in the brain. So shouldn't we take play seriously in adult life too?

I can easily lose touch with my playful self. I am a hospice chaplain and I think I have to be 'serious' (Play – P):

B Hallo.
P Hallo Bobbykins.
B I'd rather you didn't call me that please. I work in a serious place. It's a place where people die – a lot. And I'm a serious chaplain. I need you to tell me how being playful can help me in my professional work.
P Golly gosh. This is serious stuff isn't it?
B Yes it is. Now we'll have a serious conversation together.

P   Assuredly we will.

B   Excellent. I'm so pleased we understand each another.

P   I know a lovely swimming pool where we can go and have a swim together, and then we'll have a nice chat afterwards over a cup of tea and an iced bun.

B   I've got too much to do.

P   What do you have to do?

B   Have lots of in-depth conversations with people, plan some training, sort out appraisals . . .

P   Wow! Well, you do all that while I teach myself a little more on this tuba, and we'll go swimming when you've finished.

B   But then I've got to prepare for a talk I'm giving.

P   Right, stop! Stop, stop, stop, stop, stop!

B   I'm not sure I can . . .

P   You're coming with me, and we're going swimming, and we'll then drink tea together and eat an iced bun or three, and then we'll have a nice chat, and after that I'm going to laugh at you.

B   [looks puzzled]

Laughter cuts through our pomposity. Aren't we ridiculous – especially when we polish our professional personae? Jesus used a reflective device to enable people to see themselves as they really are – and perhaps to laugh at themselves too. We call it 'the parable' – a pithy story that is never supplied with an interpretation and is designed to make his hearers reflect hard in their souls. I wonder how he told these stories. We have no way of knowing, but I like to imagine him telling them playfully, with humour. He tells one story about a wealthy man who keeps pulling down his barns to build bigger ones because he is doing so well (Luke 12.16–20). He is always destroying his barns! The way Jesus tells it makes his hearers chuckle. 'And he is just about to retire and put his feet up – when he dies.' They stop chuckling.

Some years ago I wrote my own version of this story for the *Journal of Healthcare Chaplains*. It tells of a chaplain who can no longer cope with seeing patients, so he locks himself up in his office – and nobody notices. The solution to his dilemma is to become a Chaplaincy Manager – he can legitimately avoid seeing patients because he will be organizing everyone else. He becomes involved in high-level national strategies for spiritual care, and finds he is better paid and so able to afford a bigger and better car. And then one day he has a heart attack and dies. On entering heaven St Peter is very pleased to see him. 'We need someone like you', he says. 'We've just got this young motorcyclist who has come in, and we need someone to talk to him.' Some people liked my story, some did not. It was my attempt to ask questions playfully about ourselves as a body of people who aspire to be 'professional'.

Direct or indirect

We are all of a piece. What happens in our body affects our soul; what happens in our soul affects our body. Rudolf Laban was a dancer and choreographer who analysed movement. He realized that any movement we perform may be described as direct or indirect, heavy or light, fast or slow. For example, if I pick up a large mug of tea and bring it to my lips I can do so indirectly (perhaps to avoid the grasp of a small child on my lap), slowly and heavily.

We can apply his theory to any situation. I go into a room in the hospice. How do I move? Do I go in at speed, yanking the door off its hinges, or slowly, gently? I sit beside the bed of a patient. How do I sit with this person? Do I sit lightly on my chair or am I like a sack of potatoes? If I move to take their hand, do I simply grab it or do I slowly place my hand on theirs and then slowly take it away and await any reaction? If we habitually move in one way we can play with another way and see what happens.

What people are facing in a hospice sometimes seems to be intolerable (even when there is a belief about life beyond death). If your wife, husband, mother, father, brother, sister or child is *dying* in front of your eyes, it can seem as though you will not be able to survive this experience. And for the staff the cumulative experience of coping calmly and professionally with these events can seem intolerable after years of living with it. Laban's direct/indirect movement is a helpful concept for hospice. Sometimes the kindest approach is the direct one: 'I think you now have weeks rather than months to live,' says a doctor very gently to a patient. This information may be necessary so that she can put her affairs in order and work out any final things she needs to communicate to her husband with words or without words ('I love you', 'I'm sorry', 'Thank you'). At other times an indirect approach will be right, as a way of tolerating the intolerable – and the indirect approach can be a playful one. I remember a patient who had made a miniature steam engine, complete with sit-on carriages. A few days before he died, his family wrapped him up in blankets and positioned him in a chair outside his room. A friend and fellow steam enthusiast then drove his train, with a passenger waving from one of the carriages, down the road alongside the hospice as the patient looked on. The look on his face was one of sheer joy. One of our nurses has a horse, and on a number of occasions she has brought him to the hospice so that a patient who loves horses may meet him. The horse puts his shoulders into the room and the patient can say hallo to him. These two examples are indirect ways of facing death; the patients know that this is the last time they will see a steam engine or a horse in this life – but it does not require words of explanation.

I went into Paula's room on the ward. Her family had thought she was going to die the day before, but she had come back from the brink and bounced back to life again. I found Paula and her family at play. They were teasing one another, and began to tease me also. Paula showed me a very large, green plastic hand they had found in a cupboard. She told me that when her consultant next came to visit her she would bring this hand from under her bedclothes, show it to him and ask him to treat this rather nasty condition. We all laughed together.

I thought about this encounter later. When I went into the room I could have been very direct with Paula. I might have interpreted the humour in the room as a defence against the awfulness of what was happening and I could have said to her, 'I hear you were extremely ill yesterday – you almost died. How are you now?' I'm not sure what response that would have elicited. As I have said, in some circumstances a direct approach *is* necessary. But through the play and the humour, Paula was speaking to us indirectly but powerfully: 'I am still me. Treat me as a human being. It's been hell, but I'm alive today and I'm going to let everybody know it.'

Playful reflection

I am a creature of habit; I like doing things in the same way. It feels safe that way. Let us imagine that I need to see David, who is a patient on the ward. I don't want to go, but I force myself. I knock on the door and introduce myself. The family senses my unease. There is a stilted conversation and I retreat with my tail between my legs. But there is another way of approaching this. A playful approach might involve retreating into my office and having a dialogue with my fear on the computer before going to see the patient (Fear – F):

B I don't want to go and see David.
F Why not?
B Because I don't know the family and they may not want to see the chaplain.

F So they might not want to see you. What's so terrible
   about that?

B They might think I'm some sort of evangelist, trying
   to convert them.

F Yes, they might.

B And I just want to be with them.

F Oh for goodness sake, I know that!

B Don't get impatient with me!

F Well hurry up then. Spit it out!

B I don't want them to misunderstand my intentions.

F So what if they do misunderstand your intentions?

B They won't like me.

F Thank God, we've finally got there!

Having identified the nature of the fear, I can now ask to be
'held' in it. I go to the room. I find a distressed family. I stay
with them for a few moments without feeling I have to try
to do too much, and I ask if I could come back again. They
tell me that's fine. Through a playful approach I have found
a different way of being with a situation.

When I've been talking to a member of staff and we have
been discussing the challenges and difficulties of the hospice,
I sometimes finish the conversation by saying, 'Onwards and
upwards. And if we can't quite manage that, then onwards
and sideways.' A playful approach is a sideways approach.
The issues around death and dying are too enormous to
confront head on. If I say to myself, 'I am now going to
look rationally and objectively at the problem of dying and
think myself through to a conclusion', I will inevitably end
up feeling paralysed. So we have to find other ways. Our
creativity is a useful resource here, but many of us tell ourselves the story that we are not creative – we can't paint, we
can't write poetry, we'll make ourselves look foolish. We have
to find a way around this critical part of ourselves. We can
trick ourselves into being creative!

If I sit down at the piano and say to myself, 'I'm going to express my sadness', nothing much will happen. I have to take myself by surprise. So I let my fingers go where they want, discovering what they want. I may find some sadness that has been locked away. Or I may crash around on the keys and discover heaviness or anger. Perhaps my touch on the keys becomes light, and I find a quiet joy. In this way I discover more about what is happening inside me.

Set yourself up with a piece of paper and a box of pastels (or simply pen and paper). Don't have a picture in your mind. Just find which colour you are drawn to and make a mark on the paper and then another mark. If you can use your non-dominant hand so much the better. Then don't dismiss the picture that emerges. It may tell you something if you stay with it.

Take a pencil and simply write down the first words that come into your head. Don't tell yourself you are writing a poem. You are just stringing words together. Or if it is helpful to have a little more structure, you could try an acrostic. Write down the first letters of a word, for example, PAIN. Then quickly write down the words that are triggered by these letters, without analysing what you write. People – Are – In – Nature. Not very profound perhaps – or perhaps it is. The pain that I carry in my soul is a *natural* one; when we work with people in distress it is natural to discover our own pain.

Listening to our playfulness

Last summer I was staying in Luzern, Switzerland, on a retreat. I went walking each day in the mountains, and one hot afternoon came across a sign to *Wolfsschlucht* (Wolf's Gorge). Intrigued, I followed the signs until I found myself in an amazing rock-lined valley. The pines were very tall, each one forced to grow high to find the sunlight where its leaves could thrive. There were delicate patterns weaved by sunlight through the trees; it was very still. My response to the overwhelming beauty of this valley was to make a 'sculpture'. I took three large branches and made them into a tripod. Then I laced other sticks around them, balancing a flat stone on one outstretched branch. When I returned a few days later I was delighted to find the structure still intact, the valley protecting it from the wind. I decided to construct a cairn of flat stones alongside it, and the result was very satisfying.

I have discovered a great need in myself to play in this way. I need to put things together. In my office in the hospice I have made a hanging 'sculpture' out of binder-twine and discarded or natural objects. I found a black plastic spider in a hospital car-park, a smashed toy car, a rose-bud that fell from a bunch of flowers that a patient carried out from our day centre – a collection of unwanted little objects finding completeness in my sculpture. Here in this sculpture is my desire for wholeness.

It is important to recognize what happens when we play. These strong needs inside ourselves can tell us much. I recognize in the sculptures my strong desire for connection with other human beings, and connection with the feminine in particular. There is nothing at all 'wrong' with this, but I need to be aware of this desire when I am listening to another person. I will desire a connection with them. This can obviously help to form a good rapport, but I also need good boundaries.

A playful approach enables us to see what is really going on inside ourselves and also inside our organizations. It enables us to bypass the rational for a while. By approaching issues sideways instead of head on, we may see things we would not otherwise see. Then we can return to the rational. What have I learnt? What might trip me up as I listen to another person? What is my unique gift and what is my unique banana skin?

4

Depth

Connections

Let us now turn our attention to the listening relationship itself and the connections that may happen under the surface of our conversations. Do we truly connect with one another today? We may join together with others at the pub, a school concert, a university degree ceremony, a funeral or a sports match. But although we share the same geographical space we do not necessarily meet one another. Many of us communicate through email today – very convenient, but email is not terribly intimate! And the television has meant we have pseudo-meetings with a large number of people. The presenter looks into the camera and tries to convince us that he is our friend; we know deep down that this is a deception. I wonder if one reason why people are drawn to volunteer in a hospice is because they know that here is the possibility of encounters with other people that touch the depths of the soul. We long to connect meaningfully with others.

When we face our own dying, most of us will want to know that we are valued and loved. But paradoxically, as we look at our approaching death we may experience a profound sense of disconnection. We may be disconnected from our previous life, when we were healthy and capable and strong; we may be disconnected from our physical body which, in its profound changes, has become our enemy; we could find that friends, work colleagues or members of our family cannot face coming to see us; we might find that we can no longer

pray or meditate. This can amount to a crisis of identity, for
we cannot recognize the person we have become.

In Chapter 2 I described how I found myself engaged with
life again by reflecting on Ezekiel's prophecy to the dry bones
of Israel. I imagined and experienced the Spirit breathing
into the disconnected parts of myself and, just as in the
passage the bones are reconnected to each other as a symbol
of the renewal of the nation, so I found myself put back
together again.

Is it possible that when we listen to another person, a
similar process of reconnection can occur?

Communicating in the depths

When a Samaritan woman came to draw water, Jesus said
to her, 'Will you give me a drink?' (His disciples had gone
into the town to buy food.) The Samaritan woman said to
him, 'You are a Jew and I am a Samaritan woman. How can
you ask me for a drink?' (For Jews do not associate with
Samaritans.) Jesus answered her, 'If you knew the gift of
God and who it is that asks you for a drink, you would have
asked him and he would have given you living water.' 'Sir,'
the woman said, 'you have nothing to draw with and the well
is deep. Where can you get this living water? Are you greater
than our father Jacob, who gave us the well and drank from
it himself, as did also his sons and his flocks and herds?' Jesus
answered, 'Everyone who drinks this water will be thirsty
again, but whoever drinks the water I give him will never
thirst. Indeed, the water I give him will become in him a
spring of water welling up to eternal life.'   (John 4.7–14)

A well in a country with low rainfall means the difference
between life and death, and the well in this story has associ-
ations with Jacob in the communal memory. Jacob had bought
a piece of land and left it to his son Joseph. It was believed
that this well was Jacob's gift to future generations. Genesis

29 records the meeting between Jacob and Rachel at another well, where he waters her flocks; he worked for 14 years for her father so that she might be his wife, and then it seemed she was barren. These resonances lie behind the current passage; already there are the themes of generosity, loss and love.

The encounter between Jesus and the woman is not promising at the start, for the differences of gender and race fill the space between them. But then something begins to happen. As they talk together a connection is made and the Spirit flows like water ('living water' means water that flows). In the depth of the encounter there is a movement towards greater life, and love comes to fill the space between them instead of fear and suspicion. I imagine that this woman has been trapped in a series of abusive relationships with men. But the love now offered does not ask anything of her; there are no strings attached. 'Come, see a man who told me everything I ever did,' she says to her friends (John 4.29). This experience of being known in the depths of her soul results not in shame but in a movement towards greater freedom and wholeness.

When we sit with another person the conversation may stay with surface realities, and this may be what is required at that moment. But we can cultivate a willingness to go with a person below the surface reality if they so wish; we can go down into the well with them and discover some living water. What may we learn from the passage about an encounter in depth?

- There is movement. The conversation between Jesus and the woman is like an elaborate dance where each person is trying to work out the steps as they go along. The space between them increases, contracts, shimmers and is ever-changing – just like water. The skill of the listener lies in going with this flow, keeping up with it and, at times, being still so that we don't interfere with the movement.

- The well is deep. In our work we may hear expressions of terrible pain and anguish – 'Why does this relationship have to end?' 'Why does she have to die?' There may be moments when a conversation touches the unconscious depths of the speaker and the listener, and we know we are on the edge of a mystery. When this happens our silence may be of more use to the other person than our words.

- In the listening encounter a person may make themselves known to us. There is the invitation of honest speaking, and the Spirit may dance in freedom.

- Note the mutuality of the passage. Jesus was genuinely thirsty after a long journey, and the woman was thirsty for a love that did not possess her. They became two human beings sitting together who discovered that they had more in common than they first thought. In the hospice we all have a desire for life in the presence of death – patients, relatives, staff and volunteers; this is our common need. We give and we receive at exactly the same moment.

- On that particular day, as she goes to fetch water from the well, the woman does not expect life to be given to her. Her expectation is that she will avoid people by going in the middle of the day, when most sensible people are indoors in the shade. She does not go looking for a wise person to change her life! In the same way, our unlooked-for encounters may surprise us with their numinous quality. We will marvel when we hear the disconnected bones clicking back into their proper place.

- We cannot make a depth experience happen for someone. We cannot command the Spirit to dance for us. All we can do is cultivate an open attitude; we can work on ourselves so that there is more space to receive the unexpected gift.

- It is through a willingness to travel with someone to the depths that we may paradoxically discover the heights.

This does not automatically happen of course; sometimes we may need simply to stay with someone in the depths. But occasionally, without desiring it, we will find ourselves in a spacious country.

- The encounter between Jesus and the woman at the well is a lovely description of liminal space. The word liminal comes from the Latin, 'limen', which means threshold. On this side of the threshold is the world we think we know. But now and then we stumble into another sort of space where everything is upside down and inside out. We are on the edge where the sea meets the land, where soul meets spirit. In this uncomfortable space we know that we know very little. The woman in the story is off balance and out of her comfort zone; it is a state in which she can receive spiritual truth. All creative soul-work happens here in this place.

A meeting

I was cycling home one evening when my mobile phone rang. I share on-call duties for the Oxford hospitals, and a father whose teenage son was critically ill had asked to see a chaplain. I continued to cycle back home, went into the house, came out immediately with the car keys and drove to the hospital. I found a man at the end of his natural resources, who had not had enough sleep for a very long time, whose child was dying. He was separated from the child's mother.

In the next one and a half hours I listened to this man's story. Occasionally I said something, but I sensed that he simply needed to let the flood gates of emotion and speech open. I think he was a man who normally kept everything carefully controlled, but in this crisis he was not able to do that. He told me about his son's genetic disorder, about the break-up with his wife, his difficult relationship with the Church and his painful but also beautiful spiritual journey.

I was tired because it was the end of the day, and I felt hungry. But I found that I was able to stay with his conversation for the most part, prepared simply to be with him, without answers, holding on to a sense of God's love within me. When he had come to the end of his story he asked me to pray with him. I was very tired by then and I have little idea of the words I used. All I know is that they felt right and that as I prayed I felt no sense of strain or anxiety about saying the right or the wrong thing. The words were just there. I do not expect to meet this man again this side of heaven, but for an hour and a half our lives met, and the Spirit danced in the space between us.

The space between

In the above encounter I was on the edge of my functioning. Some of my usual unhelpful strategies were shut down because I was tired. How do we allow the connection with another in less extreme circumstances?

Let me consider what can get in the way of my connection with another human being: 'I think I need to perform and show that I am skilful'; 'I want a result'; 'I want to achieve something'; 'I have a need to be powerful and help.' Or the opposite may be the case: 'I feel inadequate to the task'; 'I am not good enough'; 'I am going to mess everything up'. In both cases I am likely to get in the way of the flow of the conversation and trip myself up.

But let's pause for a moment. Perhaps here is an invitation to be empty and accept both my power and my weakness so that I can then forget about them both. I need an attitude of desiring only to be with a person in my emptiness. I do not even need to desire their good, for this too can become an inward 'work'. Interior prayer may help me to find this focus. The invitation is to truly *be* with the person. I may find myself irritated with her or drawn to her or repulsed by her. I may feel profoundly sad, joyful or afraid – and I am invited to hold lightly to this awareness of my own reactions, while looking into the space between us. This space is always a loving, good space, filled with light; all I need to do is become aware of it.

I do not create this space. If I try to manufacture it, nothing will be created. It is a place that I glimpse out of the corner of my eye; it is a different land, and my task is simply to rejoice in the gift of it and marvel at the beauty of the landscape. The connection between us may be fleeting. It may consist in the exchange of a look or one phrase that sums up the person's experience. Or it may be a connection that goes deeper and deeper with successive conversations.

In this space between us I am prepared to let the other person be who they are. My desire to change them will fade. The focus is no longer on myself as a person who listens – or whether I am 'good' or 'bad' at my work. And neither will the focus be on the other person – what their story is, how they are feeling, what is important to them (although of course I will still be attending as carefully as I can to them). A shift occurs. Some will talk about the presence of God, some a dynamic energy or a spiritual charge. Both speaker and listener are taken up into something greater both than themselves and the moment. There is a connection because we have connected to that which is lovingly Other. We may be especially aware of this when someone is close to death – this is the dance of the Spirit in the space between us.

The cost

At this point I need to remind myself of something important. I can easily get carried away with the flights of Spirit – transcendence is very alluring to me. But soul and body must not get thrown out with the dirty bath-water. That was the message of the dream I described in Chapter 2 (about the young woman and our dog under the water).

Tucked away in the first book of the Bible is a strange and beautiful story that tells of Jacob wrestling with a stranger during the night. It is the account of an internal, mysterious process of transformation. Jacob is going to meet his brother Esau, and his deceptions are about to catch up with him. This will be the first time he has seen his brother since he stole the blessing and privileges of the first-born from him. He is about to cross a river – as we have seen, a powerful symbol of life and death:

> That night Jacob got up and took his two wives, his two maidservants and his eleven sons and crossed the ford of the Jabbok. After he had sent them across the stream, he sent over all his possessions. So Jacob was left alone, and a man wrestled with him till daybreak. When the man saw that he could not overpower him, he touched the socket of Jacob's hip so that his hip was wrenched as he wrestled with the man. Then the man said, 'Let me go, for it is daybreak.' But Jacob replied, 'I will not let you go unless you bless me.' The man asked him, 'What is your name?' 'Jacob,' he answered. Then the man said, 'Your name will no longer be Jacob, but Israel, because you have struggled with God and with men and have overcome.' Jacob said, 'Please tell me your name.' But he replied, 'Why do you ask my name?' Then he blessed him there. So Jacob called the place Peniel, saying, 'It is because I saw God face to face, and yet my life was spared.'
>
> (Genesis 32.22–30)

Jacob's struggle is deep within the core of his being. This is no flight of Spirit – it is demanding soul-work. He finds that there are different aspects of himself at war with each other. Darkness and light, love and fear battle it out until he emerges, *wounded*, but with a new name and a blessing. In the same way, our soul-work brings with it a cost but also the possibility of transformation. The emergent self still bears a unique wound but carries it in a different, lighter way. Now the wound can become a portal; through it we can connect with the person we are listening to, and we may even become a blessing.

In Part 2 I examine some of the reactions of my soul as I listen to others in the hospice. These will not be exactly the same as your reactions, because we are different human beings living and working in different environments. But at the same time what is personal can paradoxically have a universal reach. I hope you will find here some routes into your own lived experience so that you may discover your own unique way of soul reflection.

Part 2

SOUL REFLECTIONS

5

Sad

The layers of grief

Close to the Nuffield Orthopaedic Hospital in Oxford is an area called Cliff Edge. Here is an ancient quarry where you can clearly see the different layers of sediment laid down over millennia. A tropical lagoon used to be here, and coral once grew in the warm shallow waters. Today, fossils of shells and tiny sea creatures are clearly visible in the cliff – a mysterious reminder of a watery past alongside a very modern hospital.

When we work with sadness and distress there will be times when the pain will pierce our defences. A doctor leaves a difficult conversation with a patient and their family and needs to seek out a quiet place where he can cry. A nurse goes home and watches a film in which the central character dies; this suddenly connects with her daytime work and she is overwhelmed by grief. As well as these sudden stabs of loss, we may also discover that there are layers of sadness that have been laid down over a long period of time. The sediments of loss have formed strata of grief in the heart.

After working in the hospice for three years I found that I was feeling very sad. Sometimes, at the end of my morning reflection time, I would end up sobbing. This was not in the least unpleasant; it was quite a relief to be honestly express- ing the accumulated distress that had stuck inside me. But there was part of me that felt embarrassed about it. 'I ought not to be feeling this way,' I said to myself, 'I should not be feeling this weight of sadness.' I had thought I allowed the grief of others to go straight over the top of my head, but this was naive. Some of the distress had penetrated my heart, got stuck there and was demanding recognition. Over the three years there had been many encounters with patients, relatives and also members of staff who were coping with their own losses. I could not remember all the names and faces, but my heart still contained some of the grief.

I had also conducted many funerals and experienced that peculiar weighty sadness of a group of people grieving together. At a funeral the officiant's task is to 'hold' the ritual so that relatives and friends can grieve as they need to. This requires a lot of spiritual energy. It is not helpful for the officiant to express the sadness that is experienced, and I find I can easily push it underground into the unconscious – and more sediment is added to the strata of grief.

Professionalism and boundaries

I find it hard to acknowledge my feelings of sadness. Why is this? Let us look at some possible explanations. Perhaps I allow them to build up inside me because I think I have to demonstrate a 'professional' attitude in my work. I sometimes hear nurses who are new to the hospice apologizing for their tears, their vulnerability and their 'weakness'. I know that I expect myself to be superhuman, to work in an environment where there is huge distress without being affected by it. But if we jump into a river, it may just be that we will get wet.

I need to ask myself the question, 'What is a professional attitude?' You will have gathered already that I am suspicious of the professionalization of hospital chaplaincy. I fear that because of the detached stance we think we need to take, professionalization may lead to a distancing of ourselves from people who are hurting. True professionalism means the highest possible standards of training, work-practice and accountability. False professionalism means hiding behind role or status, thereby protecting ourselves from pain. I have often done this: I put on the persona of the professional chaplain who can cope with any situation – except that I can't. The sadness creeps under my careful defences like floodwater under the back door.

I know that boundaries are extremely important in caring work – they are part of good professional working. If we allow ourselves to be sucked into the other person's world or to become unhealthily attached to them, we are not going to be helpful. But if we are cold and detached – a professional persona with no heart, who cannot cry – then no relationship can be built and we will be just as unhelpful. We must be totally involved and totally detached at exactly the same moment – and this means walking a knife-edge.

But the task is made easier when I realize that this is the work of love. Those who care are all amateurs – literally, 'those who love'. And the loving stance is to keep a strong boundary while reaching out to the other person at the same time. I am 'holding the space' so that the other person can explore what they need to explore and be who they need to be in that moment. I am bound to be affected by this, and am not doing the work properly if I experience nothing. The sadness I feel is a consequence of my closeness to sad people. As always, it's a question of what we do with it having experienced it.

Not enough loss

Another reason for my difficulty in owning my feelings of loss is that I feel I don't 'deserve' to feel them. I can feel something of a sham working in a hospice. The bereavements I have faced in my own life are not so significant – grandparents, my mother-in-law (who did live with us for two years, and we were close), beloved dogs . . . But I have not lost a child or a spouse, I have not been made redundant or homeless and I am able-bodied.

My reaction can be, 'What right have I to be with you in your sadness? I cannot understand because I haven't been there myself.' This can make me feel de-skilled and somewhat tentative in engaging with patients and families. I think I might get something wrong, and find myself almost wanting to face a major bereavement in order to understand better what people are going through. (The opposite can also be true of course: a person who cares for others may be too close to their own grief and so not have enough internal space to be with others who are grieving.)

I need to remind myself that to be empathetic we do not have to experience exactly the same thing as another human being. All we need is an openness to human experience. We need to hear what this sadness is like, feel its contours, its heaviness or lightness. Some will be generous enough to allow us to experience with them a little of what we have not experienced ourselves. Then the patient becomes our teacher.

Encountering the sadness

I wanted to own this sadness and stop pretending that it did not exist. So I took pen and paper, placing the pen in my non-dominant hand (which helps to go below the surface to my deeper selves), shut my eyes, brought to mind my experience of sadness (trying to really feel it) and let the pen move. I found first of all that it was moving quite slowly, making spiralling movements. Then the movements became bigger as I felt more of the sadness. At first it seemed as though I were playing a game with myself, but then it became much more real. The circular movements became quicker and smaller – more intense – and I was pressing harder on the pen. By now I was really experiencing the pain of loss.

After a while I stopped and opened my eyes. What I had drawn looked like a whirlwind, spinning fast with a black centre to it. It was this black centre that drew my eye. Here was the tight knot of pain I was feeling inside me. I gave a title to the picture – *My Sadness.*

Lazarus

I am drawn to the story of the raising of Lazarus because I know I will find the Christ weeping here. In the past I have struggled with the narrative. John presents the story as a proof for the divinity of Christ and as a foretaste of the resurrection of Christ. The focus is on believing in the Son of God. I hate the contrived manner of the story: Jesus delays coming to heal his friend in order to demonstrate his power over death, so his friend has to die! How important it is to have an internal dialogue with those who evoke such a passionate response in us! I can say to St John, 'Please don't mess around with death and dying. How dare you suggest that Jesus plays around with someone's life and death just to make a point and get people to believe!' But when I get through my anger I come to a part in the middle of the story where a completely different note is struck:

> When Mary reached the place where Jesus was and saw him, she fell at his feet and said, 'Lord, if you had been here, my brother would not have died.' When Jesus saw her weeping, and the Jews who had come along with her also weeping, he was deeply moved in spirit and troubled. 'Where have you laid him?' he asked. 'Come and see, Lord,' they replied. Jesus wept. (John 11.32–35)

As I reflect on this passage I see a shift in the narrative. At the beginning Jesus is acting as a rabbi with Martha; he is teaching her that death is not the full stop that it may appear to be, and that he represents a life that is different from the material life we live on earth. But then the narrative changes, and with Martha he becomes a fellow sufferer. She falls at his feet, overcome with grief. Everyone in the crowd is weeping, and Jesus begins to sob himself. Doctrine gives way to shared grief. In my imagination I see Jesus kneeling down; Mary and Jesus cling to each other, both crying. Then with their arms around each other they go to the tomb of Lazarus.

I find Christ's connection with our pain and grief reassuring. He no longer stands on the sidelines, waiting, observing, acting independently. He is profoundly affected by the loss of his friend Lazarus. He is not the detached 'false professional' but rather the amateur, the one who grieves because he has loved. An experience of grief will often be the direct consequence of our loving. So in the end the story is affirming and life-giving for me. If Christ can weep for his friend then it is fine for me to sob occasionally at the end of my morning reflection time.

Facing our own dying

So far so good, but I think I am missing something important. Sometimes I am with a person in great distress and I simply do not wish to be there. I do not wish to share their loss and pain and I become very anxious inside. Perhaps I am in touch with the panic associated with my own dying. I may not be fully available to the other person in the encounter because I do not wish to experience through them the loss of my own life. If there is any truth in this, then my reluctance to experience the sadness of the hospice is related to my reluctance to face my death. Perhaps it is time to turn around and look death in the face (Doctor – D):

B   Hallo.
D   I'm afraid I've got some bad news for you.
B   Aha?

D The difficulties you have been experiencing are caused by a cancer, and I am sorry to say that there are no active treatments we can offer you.

B Right.

D Is there anything you would like to ask?

B OK . . . Where do we go from here?

D I will put you in touch with the hospice.

B I used to work in a hospice.

D Ah, good. So you will know the set-up then?

B Well, I know it from the point of view of a chaplain trying to offer help. But not the other way round.

D I will ask the hospice consultant, Dr Rogers, to contact you. You can meet with her and she will be able to talk with you about the help the palliative care team can offer you.

B How long have I got, would you say?

D I think we are talking about months rather than years.

I go out of the doctor's room feeling sick and sorry for myself. I cannot properly take in the news. I am numb. Will I die before Christmas? I always thought my wife would die before me, and I could be the heroic carer – this is the wrong way round. I have no spiritual thoughts whatsoever. There is no sense of calmly facing death because there is a life beyond. I am close to panic. Something is being ripped away from me, and that something is my life. I feel cheated, thwarted. I thought I was in control but it seems I am not. I won't live to see my grandchildren. I want to be grateful for my living thus far, but I just feel empty and miserable and very frightened.

I've got to tell my wife, my children, my parents. Do I want people to come and see me – friends who we've had little contact with recently? Not really. I want to hide away and lick my wounds. 'I'm going to die.'

I say it to myself over and over. But it will take a while for it to feel real.

The grain of wheat

Having accepted that I panic at the thought of the loss of my own life, I need to find a container for the panic. The symbol of the grain of wheat is a good one for me: 'Truly, truly, I say to you, unless a grain of wheat falls into the earth and dies, it remains alone; but if it dies, it bears much fruit' (John 12.24, ESV).

These words are very helpful to me. I can imagine myself as the grain: the falling is horrible; I am out of control and I don't know how far I will fall; I can't see what I'm falling into (I think this can be precisely the experience of patients with a life-limiting illness). But there comes a halt to the falling – and the end is not onto concrete with a splat, but rather into soft, warm earth; I am loved; I am held (sometimes a patient will say to the staff, 'I just want to be cared for', and hospice at its best does this); I am not on my own. As I reflect peacefully in the womb-like earth I am aware of the love of many, many people; their goodness is tangible to me; I am full of gratitude for my living and for the love and goodness of all these people. My life cracks open and the green shoot of new life appears; it thrusts upwards, seeking the sun, and there is joy.

This reflection fills me with hope and balances the panic. When I encounter sadness and loss, can I do so from this held place? Not always – sometimes it will still be from the place of panic, but now I have a little more awareness; I can see a little further along the road. I see that the fear of my own dying needs facing and befriending. This is what I need to work on inside myself.

Loss is a fact of life. Wherever we work and whatever our life experience, we cannot escape its touch. Judas kissed Christ in the Garden of Gethsemane and handed him over to his suffering. So loss will kiss us most days – in our memory and in the small and large deaths that accompany change of any sort. In our listening work we may pay attention to the hidden or obvious losses – and reflect on their impact in our soul. And when we try to face up to our own dying we are freed to live more lightly; we can breathe and be playful in our work; perhaps we will tolerate the losses of those we listen to more easily.

6

Afraid

I am in the new Cancer Centre, walking along the corridor to the oncology ward, and I would prefer to be doing almost anything other than this. I want to run away, but a sense of duty and my role as chaplain keep me moving forward. The feeling is in my guts, deep below conscious thought, and as I walk I cannot adequately describe the experience to myself. I've been asked to see a particular patient whom I have never met before. She is dying. Now I am approaching her room. I see she has a nurse with her and that there are two other people in the room. My legs take me past the room. 'I'll come back later', I say to myself. I do not want to wait. As I go past the nursing desk on my way out I catch the eye of a member of staff I know. She asks me how I am, which is kind. But the conversation that follows seems shallow and not truthful. Aware that I simply want to get away I become flustered, extricate myself and walk off the ward feeling guilty that I have not achieved what I came to do.

This experience triggers a memory from 25 years ago. I am a few years into my first appointment as a Methodist minister and I hear the shocking news that the son of my superintendent minister has been killed in a car crash. Something tells me that I have to go and see him and his wife in order to offer my condolences, but I am dreading the encounter. I have never been in a situation like this before. What do I say? How will I cope with their grief? I force myself to go, but as I walk down the path to their house I want to escape, to run away. I make myself ring the bell. The minister's wife opens the door and I say how sorry I am and give her an awkward hug. I do not know how to help; I am not sure I should even have come; every second I am there I just want to get away.

Facing the fear

I have described two experiences of fear. I am ashamed of this fear, which makes it hard for me to look at it clearly. I would prefer to tell you that I can always go about my work with confidence and that nothing at all frightens me, but the fear reaction is part of life. As a young man serving in the navy in the Second World War, my father's job was to look after the guns on a destroyer. He tells how his knees would be bruised from their knocking together during action stations. In extreme situations we face a brick wall of fear – it is huge, seems very solid, and there seems no way around it. So given the fact of our fear reaction the question becomes, 'How do we have the courage to look fear in the face and find a way through it?' Courage is acknowledging the impact of fear upon us and holding the fearful self so that we can continue to work and love. My father says he discovered that only by accepting the very real possibility of death at a young age could he get on with his job.

Let us return to the two descriptions of my fear and ask what is happening. Here are some possibilities:

- I am walking into the unknown. If I had already met the patient on the ward it would be much easier; if I had encountered a similar tragedy before it might have been easier to 'stay' with my superintendent minister and his wife.
- I want to avoid sickness, death and disaster. This is an entirely natural, primitive, survival instinct. If I am in the presence of cancer or grief I may be contaminated – I

might 'catch' cancer; I might 'catch' grief. I want to be well, whole and alive, so I will want to keep away from people who could be a threat to my well-being.

- I fear the enormous power of emotions. Will someone be out of control in their experience of anger or grief? The family I grew up in worked quite hard to keep strong emotion under control. I still suspect that strong emotion might be negative and death-dealing, therefore I want to keep well away from unrestrained emotion.

- Disease and death taste of evil. This is what I wrote in my journal after the first fearful episode:

As I walk along the corridor it is as if I am pulled down into a spiral of no-being. Creation is in reverse, and the universe is being slowly pulled apart, as a small boy pulls the wings off a butterfly. This is the opposite of the freshness of spring. It is the opposite of joyful encounter with another. This is like the jaws of an animal trap, the terrible pull of darkness against the light. I feel I have no energy to love. My presence, which is the tool of my trade as a chaplain, is a flickering light. I realize I am not going to be useful like this.

Fear in the soul

This raw fear is of course the experience of patients and families. When someone first comes into the hospice there is often an atmosphere of fear in the room. Perhaps the family has been pushed to the limits of their endurance and the home situation has become very tense. Everyone is exhausted. The patient has not wanted to come in to 'the house of death', but she has given in to the entreaties of family and professionals, and here she is, vulnerable, prised out of the familiar comforting surroundings of home, not knowing what to expect. The family do not know what to do. A succession of different professionals come to see the patient and ask her questions. They appear friendly, but they are strangers. Will this be the place where she dies, or can the symptoms be sorted out so that she can go home? This fear usually reduces in intensity as patient and family get used to the staff and the routines of the hospice; then it can become a place of safety. But the fear may return at any time.

The fear on the oncology ward feels very different. There are too many questions and too many unknowns. 'Will this treatment work?' 'What are the side effects likely to be?' 'Could I go on a trial drug?' 'What will the scan reveal?' 'Do I want to know what the prognosis is?' 'How much pain will I get and can I cope with it?' 'Will this exhaustion go on for ever?' 'Am I dying or will I actually recover?'

Examining the bricks

In the face of fear, what can I do? I need the courage to look at the brick wall of fear. It is too big to face head on, directly, but I can take just one brick in my hands and examine it in detail.

I have forgotten the most obvious thing about my fear reactions in the hospice and hospital. That is the nature of fear: it throws up a smokescreen so that we cannot think clearly. The obvious thing is that this fear has its origins way back in my childhood. As a child I had asthma and thought I would die – not of asthma but of something else. I take a brick in my hands and look at it. I convinced myself for many months that I had a brain tumour and would die. I take another brick and I see a sailing boat called *Japonica* on the Norfolk Broads. In many ways it was a delightful family holiday, but it was dominated, for me, by the appearance of a whitlow on my finger. I hugged this terrible sickly-sweet fear to myself, convinced that I had blood poisoning and would die. Eventually I told my mother, who reassured me that I was not dying, and life flooded back into my being. I take another brick and see my early fear of abandonment, cut loose from my mother, detached from the sources of love and life, a body left out for the crows and wild animals. This is the very opposite of being connected to life. As I look at the bricks there is a feeling of relief, and my current fears begin to make sense. No wonder I want to avoid cancer and death now, given that I spent whole chunks of my childhood in fear of cancer and death! As I look the fear in the face, the brick wall is not as solid as it at first appeared.

Gethsemane

' "Abba, Father", he said, "everything is possible for you. Take this cup from me. Yet not what I will, but what you will" ' (Mark 14.36). Jesus is facing suffering and death on a Roman cross. What do we learn from this confrontation with fear? Let us look at the words of the text phrase by phrase:

'Abba, Father'

For Jesus, God is the intimate Other. Abba is the natural word used by a child for his father, and the context of the anguish of Gethsemane is a relationship in which Jesus is gently but firmly held. He is bound by the ties of kinship, and I am reminded of patients in the hospice who have been loved so beautifully into death by their family. He is not alone in the darkness of the olive grove, nor does he face fear in a morally or spiritually neutral zone. The story of his connection to the Father is the environment in which he experiences fear and abandonment.

'Everything is possible for you'

Here is the counter to the downward spiral into evil and no-being. The possibilities of life, growth, wholeness and the

Kingdom are all there before Jesus. Life contracts to this speck of a moment where there is intense pain, but there is always that which is beyond this moment. When a family faces the death of a loved one, everything that is may seem to be contained in a small bubble; this room, this bed, this box of tissues, this vomit bowl, seem to be the only reality. These things become a microcosm, a tiny universe. But just beyond the room the blue tits are upside down on the bird-feeders, proving that life and goodness still exist outside the fear.

'Take this cup from me'

I hear Jesus saying, 'There is a brick wall in front of me. Show me the way around it. I'm not a death junkie; life is good. There is so much more for me to do. The disciples are not ready to go it alone. I will jump over the wall, tunnel under it. I have the energy for this.' And I hear patients and their families urging doctors to give radiotherapy, chemo-therapy, trial drugs – anything that might give a little more life. For we do not tend to cast off life easily.

'Yet not what I will, but what you will'

Again, I hear Jesus saying, 'But if you need me to, if you really need me to, and this is the right way, I will go through the wall. In fact I can see windows in it now. I didn't see them before. It is night here, but through the windows I can see a glimmer of light. If you need me to, I will go through. I will accept what has to be.'

Reading the Gethsemane account, I wonder for the first time why Jesus returns to the disciples. In the account, he asks the disciples to stay awake while he goes off to pray. But why does he come back to them? Why doesn't he just keep on praying? He could have been checking up on them, but I think it is more likely that he simply needs to know that they are still there. He needs human presence. When he comes back he finds that they are asleep, which is not great, but at least they are there.

The learning

So now I can work out what I need in the face of fear:

- I need flesh and blood people to be with me, to share the journey with. Being with others reminds me that the wall is not my only companion.
- I need 'something' beyond me and my fears. I need a transcendent yet personal Other. The context of fear is everything. It can seem that I am facing fear in a morally or spiritually neutral place, but this is a lie. I face fear as a beloved child of God.
- I need the process of reflection that puts me back in touch with, 'everything is possible for you'. By having the courage to face the wall and examine it brick by brick, I can find again the possibilities of life and growth on the other side.

Jesus in Gethsemane models acceptance, faith, courage and freedom. I can now look at my 'cowardice' on escaping from the oncology ward, understand my reaction, and forgive myself. Next time I go I can enter the room, sit down with the patient, listen and hold her in light and in goodness. The reflective process empowers me. The wall stays exactly the same, but I am subtly different.

Dialogue after Gethsemane

(Jesus – J)

B   I didn't stay awake.
J   No.
B   I think we . . . I . . . had drunk a bit too much wine at the Last Supper.

J   Last Supper?

B   That's what we call it. The Passover meal yesterday.

J   Ahh . . .

B   I wasn't coping too well with the tension and the
not-knowing.

J   Death seemed close to us all I think.

B   [gratefully] Yes. I was facing for the first time the
possibility of being arrested and . . . well, you know
the reputation the Romans have.

J   Road-builders, political wizards, creators of warm
houses in cold climates . . .?

B   I was thinking more of the torture and crucifixion
side of things.

J   Ah yes. That too! That too.

B   Are you taking this seriously?

J   Sorry. It's just that I find cracking a few jokes in the
presence of fear and calamity breaks the atmosphere
a little.

B   I didn't stay awake.

J   As you say, you didn't stay awake.

B   And I should have stayed awake. You needed us.
You needed us to watch and pray with you. And
I let you down . . . because of fear.

J   And the wine. I think you mentioned a little wine
you had drunk.

B   [in exasperation] Yes, I had drunk a little too much.
But that was because everything seemed out of con-
trol, spinning away into the dark. It was horrible.
And you seemed distant and . . .

J   Distressed?

B   You could say that. And I didn't know what I could
do about it.

J   So you went to sleep . . .

B   Don't laugh at me!

J   I'm simply pointing out the facts of the matter. No judgements. Just the facts.

B   [silence, and then] I think sleep was better than seeing your anguish and pain. I needed to shut down.

J   Yes.

B   It was too much. I was afraid of being arrested and I was disorientated because you seemed out of control. I'd never seen you break down before. You were crazy. Do you remember?

J   I remember throwing myself around a bit.

B   And we didn't know what to do.

J   I just wanted you to be there, that's all. And so you were.

I like the way Jesus doesn't take me too seriously in this dialogue; I love his sense of humour. And there is humour and laughter in the hospice, sometimes even as someone is dying. It's a good way of dealing with the fear. We remember when he was . . . and how he used to . . . and how we would . . . And people laugh together.

Fear is crying out for our understanding – and we need to hear what he has to say; he needs our hospitality too. But when we have listened carefully we can play with him. We can tell puerile jokes to him, or throw cabbages at the brick wall or really annoy him by putting on a gas-mask when we sniff the approaching smokescreen. When we can play with our fear we are set free to love.

7

Angry

When it was almost time for the Jewish Passover, Jesus went up to Jerusalem. In the temple courts he found men selling cattle, sheep and doves, and others sitting at tables exchanging money. So he made a whip out of cords, and drove all from the temple area, both sheep and cattle; he scattered the coins of the money changers and overturned their tables. To those who sold doves he said, 'Get these out of here! How dare you turn my Father's house into a market!' His disciples remembered that it is written: 'Zeal for your house will consume me.' Then the Jews demanded of him, 'What miraculous sign can you show us to prove your authority to do all this?' Jesus answered them, 'Destroy this temple, and I will raise it again in three days.' The Jews replied, 'It has taken forty-six years to build this temple, and you are going to raise it in three days?' But the temple he had spoken of was his body.

(John 2.13–21)

In the outer courts of the Temple, animals were sold for the Temple sacrifices. There is some evidence that the traders had a monopoly and could charge what they wished. Furthermore, money changers flourished because the 'unclean' Roman money had to be exchanged for special Temple coinage. Some people were making a nice profit. This is how I imagine myself in the scene:

We went to the Temple to be still and to pray. In the outer courts we had to pick our way through the sacrifices. There were pens crammed full of sheep and cattle, and cages of doves. The sellers came up, trying to convince us that their animals were the best and cheapest. Then the money changers followed us, telling us we could get the best rate of exchange with them. It was exactly like the marketplace. I looked at Jesus and could tell he was not amused. When we were inside in the cool, the sounds from outside invaded the prayer. That evening over supper Jesus told us he was going to clear the place. He said that if the soul of the nation was encumbered in this way with material interests, God could not do a new thing in our midst. We were all fearful. Someone said that if he cleared the space tomorrow, then the day after they would all be back, and so what would be the point. I reminded him of the powerful forces at work. The religious ones had allowed the outer courts to be used in this way. It was all perfectly legal. He could get us all arrested. He just smiled at me. 'Courage, Bob,' he said, 'courage and trust.' I was not reassured. I watched him plaiting some cords together and, to my horror, I saw that he was making a whip. The following day we went to the Temple at the time when crowds of people were streaming in to pray. He stood in the middle of the heaving crowd and shouted out, 'This is my Father's house of prayer!' And he started brandishing the whip. At first people sniggered. But then he opened up the pens and used his whip on the rumps of the animals. 'Clear the space!' he shouted at the top of his voice. The sellers were shocked and enraged and started shouting back at him. He ignored them and started turning over the money changers' tables. I caught a glance of him and saw the anger and passion in his flushed face. Everyone was shouting. Animals were careering all over the place, bleating and bellowing. Doves were flying up into the air. It was utter pandemonium. I thought somebody might try and grab him or punch him in the face, but I saw the fear and confusion in their eyes. You don't easily confront a prophet who is intent on giving a sign to the people! I followed him around apologizing to everyone. 'Sorry, he's a bit angry today!' I helped pick up the coins that had scattered all over the ground. I helped put a sheep back into its pen. 'Sorry everyone!' I found that I was exhilarated and terrified in equal measure.

Terrified

Anger can feel dangerous and destructive. When I was working as a chaplain in high-security psychiatric hospitals there were one or two occasions when I felt very uncomfortable because of the anger I experienced from patients. But equally I have felt very unsafe in the presence of uncontrolled anger expressed in church meetings!

Early on in my life I learnt to suppress my anger. I thought I needed to do this in order to be loved and accepted by people, and later I thought that the burying of anger was a necessary part of Christian discipleship. I believed that the frank expression of anger was wrong. I also knew the power of my own anger. On the rare occasions when I did allow my anger free rein I was frightened by the experience of feeling out of control. After these outbursts I pushed the anger down even more. The problem is that buried anger does not disappear; it just turns into passive aggression. Then everyone but you knows that you are angry!

In the imaginative sequence above I try first of all to stop Jesus from using his anger by rational argument. Later, when he is driving the animals and people out of the Temple courts, I try to appease those who are at the receiving end of his anger. I want everything to be calm and peaceful, and above all I want Jesus to stop what he is doing. I am disturbed because of Jesus' anger, and struggle to make sense of his actions. I much prefer him as Prince of Peace.

Exhilarated

But the fear of the chaos and being out of control was not my only reaction. I also found the whole event incredibly exciting. Jesus was full of passion and energy as he drove everyone out, and nobody was actually hurt. He was simply using his authority to make a point. And in effect he was saying to them, 'If you want God to return to his Temple and purify the nation, then you'd better clean up your act.' He wasn't telling them anything they didn't know, just acting it out in fine prophetic tradition. Yes, he was angry. He was furiously angry with a system that allowed profit and greed to get in the way of true faith. He was angry with the religious politicians who sold their souls daily. And he was angry that it was the poor who lost out every time. I desire this sort of anger in my heart. It is an anger that might energize me to act on behalf of those who feel they have no value in our society – those on the edge. It is an anger that can make me challenge someone who is deliberately undermining another. Anger has its place. We need its power.

Displaced anger

Anger shows itself in the hospice in different ways. A patient may well be angry with a disease process that has made him incredibly weak, disconnected from himself, exhausted and full of pain. The dependable body that has served him well for so many years is no longer trustworthy. It turns on him like a ravening beast. He has been active all his life, helping others, going from one project to another, and now he is lying in bed feeling nauseous all the time. He used to be in control of his life and now the disease is controlling him. And underneath may be a tremendous rage against life or fate or God. 'What is happening to me is wrong. Why must I suffer this slow extinction?' In his pain he may lash out ferociously at his nearest and dearest. Nothing they do for him is right. He places this existential rage onto them, and they do not know how to handle it. They just take it, because he is so ill; they cannot return the anger because they see how vulnerable he is. But they are hurt nevertheless, even if they can see that the anger truly belongs elsewhere.

Those who care professionally for people who are dying may also be the recipients of anger. A doctor may be blamed because, although she can do much to relieve symptoms, she cannot stop the dying. A nurse may be blamed for substandard care even when she has done her very best to meet the needs of the patient. And a chaplain or pastoral-care volunteer may occasionally face a verbal attack because he represents a God who has 'sent' this suffering.

On the receiving end

Occasionally I have found myself in the presence of huge anger. What are my reactions when this happens?

My brain does somersaults. I cannot think straight and my words do not come out coherently. It feels as though I am being crushed by a great weight. I have a desire to escape from the situation and I would prefer to be anywhere other than where I am. The angry person seems huge, and I feel incredibly small. I believe that the fact that someone is angry with me must mean that I have done something wrong. I want to placate the angry person so that the anger will cease. At the same time I feel aggrieved and consider myself to be innocent. I want to hurt the angry person because they have hurt me. Afterwards the weight of the anger stays with me. I need to talk to others about it in order to process what has happened and discern which parts of the anger belong with me and which somewhere else entirely.

What do I need to apologize for and what do I definitely *not* need to apologize for?

This is what happens when I talk to my anger (Anger – A):

B   I felt absolutely crushed by you.

A   You could have stood up to me.

B   Are you saying I am weak?

A   Yes.

B   You were destroying me.

A   Anger cannot kill.

B   No, but it can undermine and hurt.

A   Come on, stand up for yourself!

B   Then I would be as bad as you.

A   I'm not bad. I just have power. It's up to you to use me appropriately.

B   I hate the word appropriately!

A   That's better.

B   What's better?

A   You sounded a bit angry.

B   Stop patronizing me!

A   Excellent.

B   Stop it!

A   Anyway, you survived didn't you?

B   Of course I survived. I actually feel stronger – as though I went through a fire and out the other side.

A   There you are then.

B   It's not very civilized though – it's not very nice.

A   Nice? Who said you have to be nice?

B   I think it was my mother . . .

Niceness

In the hospice context it is tempting to protect ourselves from the awfulness of human suffering by idealizing the staff. The nurses are angelic beings who always have smiles on their faces and who never get cross, no matter how much pressure they are under. And the chaplain is such a *nice* man, so kind and understanding. The doctors are all wonderful and have the skill to take away every bit of pain and discomfort. And the volunteers give up their precious time to push round that amazing drinks trolley, and they will hold the hand of the dying person who has no relatives in the whole wide world. It's wall-to-wall niceness.

This is a fine strategy because it means we do not really have to look at death, and it protects us from the shadow side of caring. In the hospice we have different ways of understanding palliative care, we get ratty with each other because there is too much to be done and we are dog-tired, there are personality clashes, and all the time we are trying to contain death and dying that is uncontainable. A hospice is not a *nice* place, it is a real place. It is true that there are people of great compassion who work in such places, and it is true that the quality of care is usually excellent. Many people speak well of us. But we are not angels.

Anger cuts through niceness

A man with leprosy came to him and begged him on his knees, 'If you are willing, you can make me clean.' Filled with compassion, Jesus reached out his hand and touched the man. 'I am willing,' he said. 'Be clean!' Immediately the leprosy left him and he was cured.   (Mark 1.40–42)

The text reads, 'filled with compassion'. A more accurate translation of the Greek would most probably be, 'filled with anger'. There is part of me that does not want Jesus to be angry. I want him to be nice and compassionate. But let him be angry with a disease that disfigures horribly! Let him be angry with a disease that cuts people off from their families!

Let him be angry with a disease that makes them non-people with no rights and no future!

In the same way, we need to be angry advocates. We must be angry with any systems of care that fail people, with disease processes that rob people of their essential humanity, and with power structures that do not serve. And the passion of this anger can then lead us from niceness to true compassion.

The uses of anger

Anger is not bad in itself. We may use anger responsibly or irresponsibly. This is the discovery I have made as an adult. Without a proper anger towards the way dying people were treated in hospital, Cicely Saunders would not have founded St Christopher's Hospice in Sydenham, which gave rise to the modern hospice movement. This sort of passion cuts through the red tape of bureaucracy and makes things happen. Equally, anger can totally undermine confidence and destroy relationships, and it may be displaced from its true cause onto innocent people. The challenge is to use our anger wisely, with keen awareness.

8

Outside

A double divide

Some years ago when we lived in a different part of the country, my son and I arrived back home and I found I had forgotten my house keys. I was annoyed with myself and felt very silly. My wife was out and I was not sure when she would be back. We looked all round the house to see if there had been a window left open. There was no point of entry. In those days we used to hide a spare key in the shed underneath a plant-pot! I hunted for it, but it was not in its usual place. So we prepared to wait in the shed until my wife returned. It was quite cold, so every now and then we needed to go for a walk to warm ourselves up. After many hours, miserable with the waiting, I broke a pane of glass in the front door and we managed to get in. The experience of being locked out of my own home was a powerful one.

In Chapter 5 I imagined what it might be like to receive the diagnosis of a life-limiting illness. Perhaps the picture of being locked out of your own home is the closest I can get to understand that experience. Suddenly you are part of another world – the world of illness, hospital appointments, tests, treatments and the inevitability of death. The same will apply to other traumatic life events – relationship breakdown, bereavement, diagnosis of a mental illness. You are locked out of the old 'normal' world and look in wonder at people going about their everyday humdrum lives. Your family and friends inhabit the old world too – how can they understand the new one? There is no possibility of breaking a pane of glass and forcing an entry, for the old home has gone forever. You live in a totally new place now. (This is why day-care services in a hospice are so vital. People who come along understand each other; they are kin in the new place in their souls where death is becoming a reality.)

When we sit with another person who has experienced a traumatic life event and listen to their story, we face a double divide. The first divide is the distance inside the person between their new life and the old one, which can be a profound disconnection. The second is the distance between ourselves and the person. How may two complete strangers begin to communicate with each other across such a gulf? The person may say to themselves, 'What is the point of talking to you? How could you possibly understand what I am going through?' The enormous challenge for us is to communicate across, around or through this double divide, and it is important to try to make sense of our reactions when we are in this space. Sitting with and giving our attention to a person who is dying is bound to awaken in us any issues *we* may have of being on the outside looking in. I suspect that in most of us is an 'outsider'. This is the part of us that wishes to belong completely but feels isolated and locked out.

Drawing the encounter

I took out a box of pastels, tore off a sheet of practice paper and sat on the floor in our garden room, to depict a listening encounter. First, on the left, I drew myself, seated on a chair. Then on the other side of the paper, another figure, also seated. The colour I had chosen was black. Then I sat for a while and thought about the communication between us. I found myself drawing bands of colour in the space between us. These bands started off protectively around me and then moved outwards. Next, using a strong red, I drove an arrow of colour between the two figures.

This is a simple way to uncover our complex reactions in the pastoral encounter (so long as we can get out of the way enough to let our hand reveal what the soul wishes us to know!). Here the predominant and quite startling reaction, for me, was my wish to connect with the other person. As I made the mark on the paper with the red stick of pastel, there was great energy in that movement. I experienced a very strong desire to reach out across the divide. I felt uncomfortable in myself, for I wanted this communion a little too much.

It is good to want to communicate with another human being. But the strength of my reaction in this exercise reminded me that the unhealed part of myself still finds it hard to tolerate the necessary distance between two human beings. I can still be too eager to heal the divide, and if I try to I will get in the way of the communication process.

The Outsider

As a teenager studying French I needed to study *L'Etranger* (*The Outsider*) by Albert Camus. This short novel is about a man who does not display 'normal' human emotions. His mother has died and he is unmoved. He shoots a man, for no apparent reason; the sun is in his eyes and he pulls the trigger. There is no response at all in his soul.

I was shocked by this book. The apparently bleak message went deep into my inner being, challenging my Christian optimism. I hated the lack of connection, the lack of humanity, and the message of meaninglessness that I derived from it. I remember these feelings very clearly. Looking back now, I read the deep need in myself to be connected with others. I see the fear of becoming disconnected, of being an outsider.

In Mark 5.25–35 there is a story about a woman with a haemorrhage. In the Jewish society of her day, menstruation was regarded as God's curse on women for the sin of Eve; she has suffered from uncontrolled bleeding for 12 years. This woman has spent all her money on trying to find a cure and nothing has worked. She is on the wrong side of the divide – unclean, unloved, unmarried. We find her in a crowd surrounding Jesus. She should not be there as she would be contaminating those around her, but in her desperation she is trying to make contact with Jesus. Instinctively, she knows he can help her. She reaches out, touches the edge of his cloak and immediately knows that the bleeding has stopped. In that moment she belongs; the divide has been overcome.

How do I react to this account? As I pray with the passage, I notice first of all how easy it is for me to identify with the woman. I think of how she would be 'wiped out' by other people's insensitive responses to her, and how easily I have been 'wiped out' by the words of another. I understand her aloneness. And as I sink imaginatively into the experience of her healing, I am aware of wholeness, love and life in my inner being. I am no longer wiped out; I am no longer cut off.

As I sit with all these reactions I realize that there is a profound desire for the outsider in myself to be healed. Where does this outsider come from? Who is he? I think he is probably the me that struggled for breath as a child with asthma. He lies in bed, looking at the world through an upstairs window, wondering when he can rejoin that world again.

Learning from the reactions

These reactions give me some clues as to what happens in my soul when I sit with someone in order to listen to them. At times I find the distance between us intolerable. The double divide is terrible for me to experience. I will not be the outsider, and so will try to 'heal' the disconnection. I will try to appear friendly, to 'charm' the person. 'Love me, love me, love me!' cries my desperate child-self. I want the awful divide to be bridged. I cannot be left out in the cold. We *must* meet one another at all costs.

How then do I move forward, knowing a little more about my reactions to the double divide in another person? I need the outsider in me to be held, firmly but lovingly. Then I will be able to reach out safely and strongly across the distance towards the other person. The stance of other experienced listeners is very helpful to me in finding this good place.

Learning from being listened to

I have had the great fortune of being listened to by many people over the years. When I was in my late twenties and thirties I was a Methodist minister working in the community, meeting people with all sorts of challenges and different life situations. I sometimes felt out of my depth and realized I needed some training in counselling. As part of the counselling course, I needed to be in weekly psychotherapy myself. What I now realize is that I joined a counselling course, ostensibly to increase my skills in being with others, in order to be listened to.

My therapist used a couch. I would go into the basement room, sit on the couch, take my shoes off, pull myself onto the couch, arrange the crocheted blanket over my feet, lie down and wonder what to say. She was seated behind me out of my line of sight. The therapy consisted of my saying whatever came into my head and my therapist reflecting on it. There could be some fairly long silences too. She said nothing whatsoever about herself. My projections and fantasies about her were an integral part of the work. I was intrigued about her and could deduce certain things. We did not meet during school holidays and so I assumed she had children. But more than that was difficult for me to glean. I hated this. I complained once that she knew everything about me and I knew nothing about her. 'What sort of relationship is that?' I said angrily. Her answer was very succinct: 'Perhaps it is a particular sort of relationship.' I was in therapy for five years, and I remember the sessions with immense gratitude.

My therapist was a stranger looking into my world. She was not a friend, a lover, a wife, a relative or a colleague. And the distance between us was helpful. Because she was a stranger I could tell her the most intimate details of my life. She was always there; I cannot remember a time when she cancelled an appointment. She was a constant loving presence, strong in her psychotherapeutic discipline, rooted in her self.

More recently I have become involved in the world of spiritual accompaniment and retreats, and I have experienced what it is like to be listened to by members of religious orders. This is a different experience from psychotherapy: we sit facing each other, chairs angled, so that there is good eye contact. Sister Mary says very simply, 'How are you Bob?' and I fumble for some words – such inadequate vehicles for the expression of the inner life. She sits and receives what I say – whatever it is. She stays very still, rooted in prayer, grounded in her spiritual tradition, receiving my confused words as gift. And I know myself to be held in love. But I also experience *the distance* between us. She is in her space and I am in mine. I feel no invasion of my inner being. I am able to be me. In fact I feel more 'me' than I was when I entered the room.

Rooted and grounded in love

Those who listen to us well are those who do not try too hard to bridge the gulf between us. They are comfortable with the distance, but also allow something to dance in the space between us. Because the listener is rooted and grounded in love, this allows me to be rooted and grounded as well. I discover a little more of my true self. I experience the love that 'holds' the outsider and enables him to belong in the complex reality that is me.

When this happens I am able to acknowledge and appreciate the distance between myself and the person I am listening to. I am no longer desperate to make contact. I can sit in my space and allow the other person to be in their space. I can simply *be* with who they are and what they bring to the encounter. I have discovered the important truth that in order to stand in someone else's shoes I need to stand in my own first.

Two images come to me at this point. The first is of a tree. I see myself as rooted in the good ground of life itself. Sometimes when I am listening I will cross my legs as a response to some tension in myself or the other person. When I become aware of this I will then deliberately put both of my feet on the ground. I am a tree, rooted here in this moment, in this place. There is no need for me to uproot myself and move closer to the other. I am safe and loved in this space, my outsider-self calm and held. The second picture is of a ship anchored in a harbour. The other person may be 'all at sea' but I am not going to help them by pulling up my anchor and moving towards them. Let me stay where I am, appreciating the strong chain that holds me. I am rooted and grounded in love.

9

Intimate

Body responses

Although I have moved a long way, I am still at times uncomfortable about my physical being. The family I grew up in was not always comfortable about touch and *bodies*. From the Church I received the message that sex outside marriage was sinful; in fact sin seemed to be mostly about sex and alcohol! And as a young teenager in the permissive 1960s I was a great testament to the teaching of depth psychology – that what we cannot tolerate we push into the unconscious. Perhaps it is not surprising that I found myself offering for ministry in a Church where things of the spirit were considered to be of supreme importance. But healing comes about through the process of making the unconscious conscious and through facing the 'dark' within. So part of my journey towards healing has involved befriending my sexuality.

For many of us our intimate responses seem dangerous and are difficult to talk about and own. We convince ourselves that a 'professional' approach means the absence of intimate feelings. But what happens when a sexual response occurs? Transference (when the other person transfers to us feelings that belong with another person in their life, such as mother, husband or wife) and counter-transference (our experience when we have received those transferred feelings) are very powerful mechanisms. We may find that what started as a safe, caring relationship with a patient or family member now feels like a very unsafe relationship. There is an 'as if' quality about it, and this is a powerful clue that transference is operating. For example, it feels 'as if' we are lovers, when clearly not.

When reflecting on our reactions we must always try to distinguish between our own inner material and what is being projected on to us from the other person. For example, I become aware of sexual tension between myself and the woman I am listening to. How much of this is coming from me? At a basic level I may really 'fancy' this person; or at a deeper level perhaps there is something unresolved here in my own soul. But some of my reaction may originate in the other person. For example, in the presence of the death of her husband, this woman may (unconsciously) see me as a new mate and protector.

What happens when the boundaries feel shaky and we know we are on dangerous ground? The safest way to deal with such responses is to own them, share them with someone we trust outside the situation or take them to supervision – and seek to understand them lovingly. It is important to remind ourselves that a reaction is not the same as acting something out. In this situation, as at no other time, we need to be firmly rooted in our own space where we know we are loved. And it may be that our most uncomfortable reactions are the ones that contain the most treasure. A strong feeling is not a bad feeling. It is a reaction seeking understanding.

The anointing of feet

Just before Jesus faces his final crisis he is with friends in a safe place. This is a precious time of intimacy:

> Six days before the Passover, Jesus arrived at Bethany, where Lazarus lived, whom Jesus had raised from the dead. Here a dinner was given in Jesus' honour. Martha served, while Lazarus was among those reclining at the table with him. Then Mary took about a pint of pure nard, an expensive perfume; she poured it on Jesus' feet and wiped his feet with

her hair. And the house was filled with the fragrance of the perfume. But one of his disciples, Judas Iscariot, who was later to betray him, objected, 'Why wasn't this perfume sold and the money given to the poor? It was worth a year's wages.' He did not say this because he cared about the poor but because he was a thief; as keeper of the money bag, he used to help himself to what was put into it. 'Leave her alone,' Jesus replied. 'It was intended that she should save this perfume for the day of my burial. You will always have the poor among you, but you will not always have me.' Meanwhile a large crowd of Jews found out that Jesus was there and came, not only because of him but also to see Lazarus, whom he had raised from the dead. So the chief priests made plans to kill Lazarus as well, for on account of him many of the Jews were going over to Jesus and putting their faith in him.

(John 12.1–11)

Jealous

I have found this story very helpful in my thinking about intimacy. First of all it is important to note the connection between intimacy and dying. The loving, intimate actions of Mary are overshadowed by the threat of death to both Jesus and Lazarus. Perhaps the connection is not surprising as sex and intimacy are about reproduction, connection and new life – a healthy response to the separation and apparent finality of death. Similarly in the hospice context we should not be surprised to find sexual and intimate responses occurring in the face of death and dying.

In the account, my attention is drawn to Judas' reaction to the intimacy between Mary and Jesus. His outburst changes the atmosphere, and my guess is that as he witnesses the closeness between Jesus and Mary he is jealous. *He* wants to be the centre of attention; he wants *his* feet to be anointed. 'You're wasting it on *him*?' he says to himself. Perhaps Judas has felt on the edge of the group for some time. He wants to be loved like Peter, James and John, who seem especially close to Jesus. Perhaps he experiences this act of intimacy as one more rejection. Soon he will hand Jesus over to suffering.

I understand Judas' reaction. As someone is dying I walk softly into the room and gaze on a scene of intimate connection and rapt attention; everyone is listening to the person's breathing, watching the chest go up and down. Love is gently and beautifully expressed. And at some deep level under the surface of conscious thought, I desire the love and attention being lavished on the dying person. I want my feet massaged by a lovely complementary therapist. I want people to speak tenderly about my life. I wish to be wrapped in a duvet of tender concern. Yes, I do not wish to own up to it, but I am jealous. The outsider in me wants to belong and be cared for.

This is an important insight for listening work. Intimacy includes, but it can exclude as well. When we go into a room, we need to note who is close to the bed and who is not. We may see one sister apparently engrossed in a book or magazine while the other sister holds her father's hand, looking lovingly into his eyes. What might this mean? And who is absent altogether? Family rifts are not uncommon; might there be a chance of reconciliation at the end of life so that the whole family shares in a precious intimate time together?

Intimacy can be very natural

In an imaginative reflection I picture Jesus at Bethany after the meal they have shared together. Jesus breaks down in the face of his own dying. He is among friends and can release the emotions that have been building up for such a long time. The disciples, myself included, gather round him, holding him, as he sobs out his fear and his sense of impending loss. This becomes the context in which Mary goes to collect the perfume in order to anoint his feet. In this reflection, I belong; I am part of the group, offering my love and presence. This too is part of my experience in the hospice. A woman whose mother is dying needs someone to stay with her. The woman and I sit either side of the bed, holding her mother's hands; these are precious moments of tender care, and we touch depths and heights together.

What would happen if I imagined myself in the place of Mary of Bethany, anointing the feet of Jesus? What would it reveal about my attitude towards intimacy?

B   I don't want to anoint your feet, Jesus.

J   That's OK. Do you know why not?

B   It feels like a thing a woman should do.

J   And you don't want to do a womanly thing?

B   I'd feel stupid and embarrassed.

J   Like you do sometimes in your work at the hospice?

B   Yes, I suppose so. I can feel stupid and embarrassed. I want to be properly close to people, but I don't always feel comfortable. Like today, holding Tom's hand. He was fine with it. But I felt awkward – especially with his wife looking on.

J   Do you want to try anointing my feet, just a tiny bit?

B   How can you anoint someone just a tiny bit?

J   Just for a moment then.

B   OK. [I begin to anoint his feet and stop]

J   What's it like?

B   I feel uncomfortable and a bit scared.

J   Scared?

B   Scared that I will be too close. Scared that I will overstep the mark and be told off for doing something wrong ...

J   How about thinking of my love towards you and towards everyone, and then anointing my feet?

B   [I anoint his feet again] That feels OK. I'm aware of your life and love and as I anoint your feet I give thanks for all of my relationships ...

Touching

We live in a culture where there is great openness about sex. There is easy access to pornography, advertising uses sex to sell products, and a lot of women's fashion is designed to titillate. We might assume, therefore, that we are comfortable with our bodies and with physical contact. But the British today seem to be ambivalent about touch. This is especially clear with regard to children, where all touch is regarded as potentially predatory and dangerous. What is more, men and women no longer know how to greet one another socially. Do we shake hands, kiss on one cheek, kiss on both cheeks, have no contact at all and just say hallo . . . ? We have lost the rituals and do not know how to behave towards one other.

But in a hospice touch is vital, and we need to work with any fear of intimacy. Holding someone's hand can be such a valuable bit of communication. It conveys more than words. It says, 'You are not alone, you are valuable, you are loved.' We need to be careful, of course, because not everyone wishes to be touched. Some people have been hurt badly in their relationships; they need loving presence rather than physical contact – this is the only way they can be in their dying. (There may also be physical limitations, such as fragile skin or injuries. I once put my hand on a patient's shoulder, forgetting he had broken it – he winced in agony.) But for some who have never allowed themselves to be close to another human being, the comfort of touch might be a revelation in their last days.

I cannot assume that I know how to hold a person's hand in a helpful way. It is something to be learnt. Perhaps we should role-play it in training! One danger is an imbalance of power. By holding someone's hand I might give the impression that I am the all-powerful carer: 'I'm healthy and not dying and in my infinite goodness I have deigned to hold your hand – you who are weak, afraid and near to death.'

The ideal situation is when the person takes *my* hand. In order to allow this to happen I might briefly place my hand over theirs (this indicates that I am happy to have physical contact if they wish) and then withdraw it and place it near; then they can easily take my hand if they wish. My hand must not trap theirs; the other person must always be free to withdraw it easily if they want to. I need to remember that holding hands is what lovers do, so when holding hands with a woman I need to do so in a way that conveys care and concern rather than romantic attachment. This usually means a matter-of-fact, gentle grip.

Occasionally someone will cling to me. They will hold my hand very tightly and want reassurance and answers from me. This can feel like the grip of a drowning person, and I need to remain calm and solidly anchored in myself, so that I do not join them in the drowning.

Just as people do not automatically know how to greet one another anymore, so we do not always know how to behave when a member of our family is dying. Fear of disease and death (or of intimacy) can sometimes prevent family members from being physically close to their loved ones. By holding a patient's hand, a carer may model an intimate form of communication for them. We can also encourage the family to talk to the patient, even though they may not appear to be responsive in any way – hearing is the last sense to disappear.

The boundary and the bridge

In the hospice we will sometimes be present at intimate moments between family members, lovers and friends. In the reality of dying, people often become more 'real'. They open up and express the beauty of their innermost being. Tenderness and love are shown by family members and friends, and come from a very deep place. Our privilege it is to be alongside people who are vulnerable and cracked open by dying or grief. In these situations it is natural to hold someone's hand or to offer a hug. This closeness will affect us, sometimes in a profound way, and may evoke tenderness, caring feelings or sexual responses in us.

When powerful reactions are present, it is vital to keep the boundary between myself and the other person. The 'as if' quality of the response that I referred to above needs to be recognized. I can remind myself that the person I am hugging is not my father, my mother, my sister, my lover, my husband, my wife or my friend. My role is that of chaplain. And I can remind myself that I have an intimate life that happens elsewhere and is totally different from this particular relationship of care and listening.

At the same time, a bridge can be formed. I may become aware of beautiful, profound connections that are full of goodness. These may be between myself and the person I am listening to, between the person and God or between different family members. I preserve the boundary and at precisely the same moment I am aware of the possibility of a bridge being built. When I stay anchored in this connected self I can reach out with compassion and not be afraid of intimacy.

Safe

The way to keep pastoral relationships safe is not to avoid all physical contact or to try to avoid all situations where transference might operate, but to be prepared to work on our reactions. Intimacy is one area where I know I need others to help me understand what is going on. I am then held safely in the complicated feelings I experience. And the other way to deal healthily with intimacy is, of course, to develop an intimate relationship with God, for ultimately he is the one I desire; he is my lover.

10

Tired

Recently I was sitting in a meeting feeling sleepy. I was not very much involved in the proceedings and felt myself nodding off. Because it was a small gathering it must have been very obvious to everyone in the room, but my colleagues were too polite (or embarrassed) to mention it. It reminded me of my time as a minister working in the community. I used to visit an elderly lady in her flat. She enjoyed talking and my task was to listen, but the flat was very, very warm and I would occasionally doze off as she talked. I am not sure if she noticed, but it is not something I am proud of. I also remember a visit to my spiritual director many years ago. He was obviously extremely tired, and as I talked to him his eyes became heavy and he was struggling to stay with me as I talked about my inner life. I remember being very angry with him. Staying awake matters. When we are sitting with another person, we need to try to give them our full attention; an alert and gentle presence is at the heart of all listening work. Understanding our tiredness is therefore important.

Why so exhausted?

What are the roots of the tiredness I sometimes experience? At times it will simply be the result of lack of sleep, but I believe that our tiredness is often related to the state of our inner being, and may be a psychological and spiritual response to our dis-ease. I also think that different sorts of tiredness have a different feel to them that can give us clues as to the root of our tiredness. Let us consider some possibilities:

- It may be as simple as not sleeping long enough at night-time, and not being as young as I used to be (and let me not ignore physical causes of tiredness that might need a visit to the doctor).
- My tiredness is a natural response to the distress and anguish that is present in the hospice, especially on the ward. The hospice is a container for a huge amount of human pain, and some of this pain inevitably rubs off on me. This tiredness feels weighty, expressing the 'heavy' nature of the experience of patients and families.
- My tiredness is the result of putting something to sleep within me that is uncomfortable. Patients may choose to sleep instead of actively face their dying, and so sleep is a very effective avoidance technique. It is so much easier to sleep life away; to 'turn your face to the wall'. My tiredness may be saying, 'I am scared of being with those who are dying, and I am scared of my own dying; if I just go to sleep it will all go away.' This sort of tiredness feels like an anaesthetic.
- My tiredness is because of unresolved internal conflicts. When I wrote the first draft of Chapter 9, on intimacy, I was staying in a retreat centre. I wrote about intimate reactions in the morning, and by lunchtime I felt exhausted. After lunch I lay down on my bed and slept much longer than I intended. I suspect that because the issues around intimacy and sexuality are not yet fully integrated into my self, the 'manager' of my personality wished to disallow the airing of the subject, which led to tension and tired-ness. This has a sickly feeling mixed in with it.
- I am tired through relating to too many people. My per-sonality type is on the cusp of introversion and extrover-sion. An introvert finds energy by being on their own, an

extrovert through contact with other people. I am enough of an introvert to find time with too many people draining. A power-nap of ten minutes after lunch is a wonderful escape from people and restores some of my energy.

- It may be simply that the balance of my life is out of kilter. Perhaps work takes over and I do not allow enough recovery time. The times when I walk down to the river in order to sit, watch and listen are precious times. Sometimes family life, which contains stresses, combines with work pressures – the resultant tiredness is inevitable. This sort of tiredness has an empty feel to it.

- Sometimes I drive myself too hard. Instead of letting the day flow, I will force myself along, anxiously trying to 'achieve'. I do this to try to please those in authority and to keep my guilt about not 'doing' enough at bay. This tiredness leaves me feeling drained of life because I have not been going with life's flow.

- Lack of clarity about my role – role confusion – can make me tired. Who am I as a chaplain? Am I a counsellor with some religious and spiritual bits added on, or am I an ordained minister with some counselling skills? It is tempting to think of myself as incompetent when faced with the competency of other professionals whom I respect greatly.

- Finally, I think that trying to be a professional chaplain – in the false sense of being professional – takes its toll, as I have discussed in Chapter 5. To be the detached observer of another person's suffering is tiring. The times when I can be myself and throw myself into a situation without inner reserve are actually times when I will find myself tired in a good way, but not drained or exhausted.

Just looking at the above list makes me want to go and have a nice lie-down! But instead let us look at some of these possible explanations in more detail.

Bringing tiredness home with me

Patients in the hospice are usually fatigued. They will have experienced some combination of radical surgery, radio-therapy and chemotherapy, pain that has been difficult to control, hallucinations, constipation, breathlessness, nausea, profound sadness and loss, a sense of meaninglessness, anx-iety around their own death and dying, anxiety for their loved ones and a sense of disconnection from their past life. In the face of this suffering, no wonder they are exhausted. And tiredness too is etched on the faces of relatives and friends. Theirs is a different journey. Their exhaustion may be the result of physically caring for their loved one over many months with little sleep. In the final stage of living, the challenge is to wait lovingly but helplessly with that loved one, who is slowly disappearing from view.

Sometimes in the evening I will cycle home, sit down in the living room and fall asleep. Part of this tiredness belongs to me and part of it does not; I have collected some of it from patients and families during my day. It is a heavy weight, and the sleep does not really refresh me.

This sort of tiredness is asking for particular responses. Underneath the tiredness is helplessness, anxiety and despair; understanding this enables me to discover the way through. I may respond to the helplessness by an activity such as mowing the lawn or cleaning my bike. Returning to my body helps me to create a necessary distance from the paralysing feelings; I can claim back some energy through actively doing something. I may then return to the feeling of helplessness if I need to, having found some space to 'breathe'.

The anxiety is different and requires special attention. I can choose to have a conversation with it (Anxiety – a):

b   Hallo.
a   Hallo.

B   Do you want to tell me something?

A   I wonder if I've done enough today.

B   It's OK. You sat with Jane, you laughed with Sid, you lit a candle for Ethel.

A   But the stuff they are facing is so enormous . . .

B   I know. But you were there.

A   I want to do more.

B   You are not God. You are a channel.

This sort of dialogue can re-energize me in a surprising way. When the anxiety is given the attention it is seeking, it no longer clamours in the heart.

And the despair can be met with creativity. I find playing the piano in a free way is a powerful way of expressing the deep inner material I bring home with me. Occasionally I will sing out what is in my heart as I play (more difficult because I want it to sound 'good'). I also find writing a great release. When we are creative, even when expressing difficult or negative material, we are acting in a hopeful way, receiving the life-giving energies of the Creator.

Jonah asleep – role confusion

In the Biblical narrative from the Old Testament, Jonah is a man on the run from God. He knows he needs to go to Nineveh and face his future there, but he goes in the opposite direction and boards a ship. He goes below deck and sleeps a deep sleep. No wonder – he is running away from himself, and the inner conflict is tearing him apart. The external storm is a mirror image of the internal storm. This is a conversation with Jonah:

B   Jonah! [no response, so louder] JONAH!

J   Go away!

B   I want to help.

J   Then go away.

B   I think I understand what's going on.

J   Good for you. Now get lost!

B   No, listen. It's about being in the right place. You're not in the right place – that's why this storm is happening.

J   [suddenly weeping] I can't do it. I can't do it.

B   You can't do what?

J   I can't do anything anymore.

B   Yes you can.

J   [petulantly] Can't!

B   Listen! If you don't listen to me they're going to throw you overboard and you're going to be swallowed up by a great fish.

J   Whale actually.

B   No, the text says a great fish ... The right place is not about geography. It's not about here or there – the right place is inside you. It's where you're no longer running. It's where you stop still and say, 'This is me.' For better or worse, 'THIS IS ME!' You can't run from yourself for ever.

J   For God's sake leave me alone and let me sleep.

This encounter with Jonah is fruitful and takes me further on the journey of understanding my tiredness. Jonah suffers from role confusion – the ordinary man who wants a quiet life pulls against the prophet who knows what he must do as the instrument of God.

I have been aware of my own role confusion for a long time. As a Methodist minister I am one of John Wesley's preachers, called tirelessly to offer the transforming gospel of Christ to all, that they might be saved. This person must be serious, obedient to a higher cause and, above all, holy. He wears a clerical collar. But as a chaplain I have another identity, as a non-directive listener, facilitator and spiritual companion. This person is a friend to fellow travellers and would never dream of trying to convert someone to the Christian way. He does not wear a clerical collar. The pull between the two roles is one that can wear me out. The Jonah-self descends below decks and simply puts the conflict to sleep. This is not a very creative solution!

The experience of feeling de-skilled and useless is common among those who offer care to others. In the dialogue, Jonah cries out, 'I can't do anything anymore.' This is the part of me that has lost confidence in my ability to fulfil any role, and is the final logic of role confusion. But in fact, contrary to expectations, I am now standing on hopeful ground. My true self (or true parts of the self that I do not yet fully acknowledge) beckon me onwards. Through this sense of 'not being able to do anything', I am invited to gently face the hurting part of myself that protests his impotence. The Jonah-self turns out to be the child within who is scared of the world; he is little and does not believe in himself. Only through paying attention to this self and loving him can true confidence and compassionate action come into being. Then the self wakes up, stretches in the sun and finds he has renewed energy.

By playing with the Jonah story I discover the 'right place' beyond roles and expectations, and am now free to redefine myself as an imaginative listener. This person is held in God's light and love and is able to hold others gently in God's light and love. He is a person in relationship with the intimate Other.

> May all that I am
> My darkness and my light
> My fear and my desire
> My body, mind, soul and spirit
> Be held in your love
> That I might reach out to the other.

In this relationship I do not need to sleep. Staying awake is much more fun!

Driving myself too hard

Tiredness also comes from pushing myself to achieve. I put in long days and do not allow myself enough recovery time. Of course, a long working day does not necessarily mean efficient working. I have noticed that if time is limited and I am functioning well, I can get through a lot of good-quality work, whereas if I am pushing myself remorselessly hour after hour I can lose my way. And when I am driving myself hard I can get annoyed because nobody in the hospice seems to notice (perhaps because they too are driving themselves and are too tired to notice my heroic efforts!).

Some time ago I was planning to recruit more volunteers to our pastoral team so that we could develop the service in exciting ways. We could send volunteers into the community to work alongside our specialist community team; we could go into the Cancer Centre and support people with life-limiting conditions; we might follow up patients who leave the hospice to go into nursing homes. I was drawing up a timetable for recruiting, interviewing and training this new group of volunteers – but I knew it did not feel quite right. When I am tired I am less likely to trust these subtle intuitions; I tend to plough on regardless.

My wife and I went on holiday to the Isle of Wight, and while out walking one day on the Downs, feeling wonderfully relaxed, certainly not intending to think about work, I suddenly thought, 'Why on earth am I planning to put myself under huge pressure by recruiting six more volunteers this autumn?' I realized I was pushing too hard and that the plan was not something I really wanted to put into practice at that time. I saw that my motivation had been to prove my effectiveness as part of the hospice team. So I resolved to take my foot off the accelerator pedal, and immediately found a sense of relief and peace. When I told our senior manager and clinical director that I did not intend to recruit more volunteers in the autumn, they had no difficulty accepting that decision. Members of the current team also expressed relief when I told them. We are now allowing the service to grow naturally rather than force growth.

As always, the invitation is to see behind the behaviour. It is very tiring trying to make things happen. I screw up my energies into an anxious ball – and here at last is the image that helps me understand what is really going on: my energy does not flow out; it turns in on itself because of the all-too-familiar anxiety. And what is the root of the anxiety? A desire to belong, to be approved of and to be liked.

Something shifts when I hear the voice of this part of the self, and accept that he is part of me. He only causes trouble when I deny his existence. Instead of driving myself, turning inwards into an anxious ball and becoming exhausted, I can allow my energy to flow gently out to others and the Other. I find I can move with the flow of grace and life. Sometimes it seems like flicking a switch! Instead of anxiously trying to make things happen in my day, I allow situations and people to come to me. Of course there will be problems to be solved and challenges to be faced, but they will be encountered with love, not fear. And the tiredness I feel is very, very different: it is the sort of tiredness that comes from having had a full and satisfying day.

11

Recognize me

I was only trying to be helpful

I want to be helpful and useful to my fellow human beings, and sometimes I can take this a little too far. I once picked up a hitchhiker who spun me a harrowing tale about his wife, who had been taken ill and was in a critical condition in hospital; he told me that he was a long way from home without any resources, desperate to find a way of getting to see her. As we travelled along we chatted amicably and I noticed that, considering his wife's circumstances, he was remarkably relaxed and free of concern for her. I realized fairly quickly that his story was a fabrication, but before I dropped him off I still stopped at a cash machine to help him on his way.

The inner helper is a strong motivating force for people in caring roles – without it we would not involve ourselves in caring work – but sometimes this helper wants to be a little too helpful. For a long time I wanted to be more useful to the nursing team on the ward at Sobell House. I was aware of the tremendous pressures they were under and wondered if I could be an extra pair of hands when things were very busy. Sometimes I am with a patient who has slipped down in bed and needs lifting back up, or who needs help moving from bed to chair. I could not help out because of health and safety regulations, but wondered if I might receive some basic training. This would be a way in which the chaplain could, now and then, offer some very practical staff-support.

I talked with my line manager about the idea, who agreed that I should enrol on a manual-handling training course. I emailed the training department, explaining what I intended and was given the dates. Some weeks later, feeling a little apprehensive, I arrived for the half-day's training. After waiting for 20 minutes while the trainers attempted to set up the projector for a presentation, we were asked if we were all involved in clinical work. I explained I was a chaplain hoping to increase his practical skills, and was asked to talk with one of the trainers outside the classroom. She quizzed me as to my intentions, asked if I had contacted occupational-health authorities about the change in my role and if I had talked to my manager about it. Finally she said I was on the wrong course – this course was for those with existing skills, and I should rebook on the one specifically designed for clinical support workers. I was sent on my way.

What were my reactions? I felt humiliated and angry – although I was polite with the trainer. I went back to the hospice and, telling my story in the ward office, banged my head on the table in mock (?) rage. 'I was only trying to be helpful!' I exclaimed. I felt thwarted and stopped in my tracks. More anger and indignation followed when I received an email from the training department telling me that in my role as chaplain I should not be attempting to move patients at all, and that they were unwilling to allow me on *any* sort of training course.

Such a strong reaction deserves investigation. What lies beneath it? When I thought about the encounter with the trainer in the corridor and 'hovered' over the feelings in my mind, I began to discover something very interesting. I wanted to say to her, 'You are not letting me be the good person I want everyone to see.' By helping out on the ward in a new way I genuinely wanted to be helpful. But part of me wanted everyone to *recognize* how helpful I was being.

The inner helper wanted everyone to see how incredibly generous he was being. A strong need for affirmation is uncovered through this little act of reflection. It is always worth digging when we experience a strong reaction like this – the result is always illuminating, even if we do not particularly like what is revealed!

Pushing the lorry

When I am not living out of my true self I can put myself under huge pressure to prove how useful I am. I will look at the list of patients on the ward and feel guilty because I have not visited them all. Or if I *have* seen them all I will then think I haven't had in-depth, probing, therapeutic and spiritual conversations with them all! If I am in the day centre drinking tea, eating cake, joking and chatting with the patients, I can feel guilty because I haven't been 'working'. Part of me says that it is only by working ferociously hard that I will prove my worth to the hospice and receive the affirmation I crave. I want to show everyone that I am a useful member of staff, doing extremely valuable things.

I often go on retreat to North Yorkshire. St Oswald's Pastoral Centre is in the village of Sleights near Whitby. There is a treacherous hill called Blue Bank winding up out of the village on to the moor. At its steepest the gradient is one in four, and there have been many accidents on it. If I get up early in the January darkness I will often watch the headlights on the hill. If I bring to mind the attitude of trying too hard to be useful, I imagine pushing a lorry up this hill. The effort is incredible – this attitude is full of tension and unhappiness. I feel that I *have* to do so many things. And the more I seek appreciation and recognition, the less likely I am to receive them – my efforts are untruthful and shallow, my conversations stilted and somehow wide of the mark. If, by contrast, I stop pushing and allow life to come to me, then often remarkable and lovely things happen. I find myself communicating with people I had no idea I would meet, and the encounters have depth.

A little archaeology

I can find it hard when a patient does not wish to see me. I go around introducing myself to patients and relatives: 'Hallo, I'm Bob. I'm the chaplain here. I just wanted to say hallo.' There are many reasons why someone may not wish to talk with me. Many other people may have wanted to talk to this person and ask them questions; they may simply be exhausted and without the resources for a conversation at that moment; they may be angry with life/God/fate/the Church/clergy; they may be desperate to go to the toilet; they may be in considerable pain. But a part of my self may well respond with, 'They don't want to see *me!*' I feel pushed away, unappreciated, unknown. As I write, I find this admission very uncomfortable. I need to remind myself yet again that it is important not to judge my reactions – they are simply worthy of further thought.

Let us do a little more archaeology. One method is to ask ourselves, 'When I am feeling X (in this case lack of recognition), is there someone's face that I see or a person I think of?' When I asked myself that question, I thought immediately of someone I feel has not really appreciated and understood me. So I wrote a dialogue between myself and this person. I talked to him about key events in my life and imagined him responding. His voice became that of a wise counsellor. He said to me, 'Bob, I'm very proud of you.' In writing, I experienced the encouragement and validation that he has sometimes found difficult to express. This may sound like make-believe, escaping into a fantasy world, but for me there was truth in the writing.

Another exercise was far more difficult for me: could I tell myself how much *I* appreciate me? After a morning feeling competent in the hospice I wrote the following:

> I appreciate the way in which I stayed with Jack this morning, following the journey of his conversation. I appreciate the skill I have developed in helping him to find God in his experience. I appreciate the way I 'summarized' for him, enabling him to be held in what he was saying. I appreciate his gratitude – the way in which he thanked me genuinely for the conversation. I receive that and accept it as a gift.

It is interesting how difficult I find it to transcribe this from my journal – I immediately want to explain that I am not blowing my own trumpet, that this is not pride. How difficult – and important – it is for those of us who have been brought up in a Christian culture to acknowledge that we are good fragments of creation, and that by appreciating our selves we are giving glory to the Creator!

Being recognized

I think we need to relish those moments when we are affirmed by another person. When I was at sixth-form college I was walking along a corridor one day when my French teacher approached from the opposite direction. He grinned at me, and in that grin I experienced such welcome that I have never forgotten it. Much more recently I met a fellow chaplain who I hadn't seen for eight years. He smiled and reached out his hand to me. The moment contained such warmth and joy; I was glad to be recognized and remembered by him.

I was attending a chaplains' conference. We had a free afternoon. After sleeping for an hour to catch up with myself, I went out on my bicycle. I had no clear idea where I was going, but I knew I wanted to pray and how I wanted to do it. It was not cold, but clouds were ominously dark overhead. I saw a sign to a church and followed it, only to find the church locked. Undeterred, I sat down on a step and listened to the birdsong. (I now suspect the birds were telling one another a storm was coming!) I thought about Mary Magdalene coming to the tomb on the first Easter Sunday morning, carrying her heavy load of ointments to anoint the body of Christ (John 20.1–18). I imagined the sense of loss and emptiness in her heart. (There was a clap of thunder and the birds became even more vocal.) She came to the tomb and it was empty. Christians tend to associate the empty tomb with joy and wonder, but Mary experienced a second abandonment. She could not even tend his dead body, for someone had removed it. 'Why have you left me?' was the cry of her broken heart. (The rain comes. I have to move and shelter under some thick bushes. Hail bounces on the path.) I skip in my mind to watch Mary meeting the 'gardener'. She pleads with him to tell her where the body of Jesus has been taken. 'Mary,' he says. 'Rabboni (Teacher),' she replies, recognizing Jesus and knowing in that instant that she is also known by him. I try putting my own name into the story in place of Mary's. 'Bob,' he says. What do I say to him? 'My Lord' seems to fit best. (The storm has hurried off and the sun has returned.) I stand, enjoying the sensation of the sun on my face. I am aware of being recognized, loved and held. I feel very peaceful. Outside the locked church I imagine Jesus saying to me, 'I love you not for what you do, but for who you are. You can receive more from me you know.'

Finding other sources of appreciation

I often listen to patients in the hospice who are struggling with their lack of ability to live a 'useful' life. A woman has spent much of her life caring for other people. She has given herself tirelessly for a relative or as a professional carer, and now finds herself being cared for. The tables are turned. She is demoralized and cannot recognize herself in this new situation. Or a man has achieved much in his professional life, having the respect of his colleagues, making far-reaching decisions and attaining status in his particular field. Now he is dying. He is no longer productive, no longer needed by the society that once gave him wealth and honour. Who is he, now that he cannot define himself in terms of his usefulness? In such people there is often a great desire for appreciation, recognition and affirmation.

My task when sitting and listening to another human being is to honour that person, to value their uniqueness, to relish their story and to stay with their pain and joy. I am there to encourage them by my presence. Their task is to be themselves, or as close to it as they can get in that moment. Their task is definitely *not* to make me feel special and valued and appreciated, but if I am tired and miserable, given all that I have said about my need to be recognized, I may unconsciously want just that. Then the danger is that I may spiral down in the awfulness of a need that cannot be met. I am unable to meet their need for appreciation because I am looking for appreciation myself. And I have nothing to give.

But before I give up and go home, despairing of any fruitful encounter, there is a way through. The very act of understanding my need for appreciation and digging away at the roots of that need puts me in a different place. By playing in a reflective way with this need, I take much of the power out of it. And I need to give myself permission to find appreciation from sources outside of the listening encounter. Ultimately I desire recognition from the Other who we name God. In my best self I know that I am the beloved of God, as is every other human being. As I sit with this person, listening to their story, aware of their need, I hold fast to the belief that God knows me, values me, sees me. This is not an intellectual belief, like believing a creed or a doctrine of the Church. It is the knowledge that my soul is loved. This is *intellectus* rather than *ratio*, as explained in Chapter 2. When I am in touch with this flow of life, the question of being appreciated or recognized by the other person is irrelevant because I am in that moment recognized by God.

Listening from this place, something interesting happens. I hear the need for appreciation in the other person; I hear the desperation, the longing and the sadness. But I do not need to spiral down into my desperate need for recognition because I know I am recognized. Listening from this new place of life, my unspoken message to the other person becomes, 'You matter because of who you are, not what you have done; you matter because you are you.'

12

Fix it

Studies in frustration

I remember a young man who was dying in the hospice. During the time he was with us I got to know his mother reasonably well. But her son did not wish to engage with me because I think I reminded him of his own death. After all, clergy are people who say prayers with the dying and lead funeral services, and he was not ready to think about that. I saw him quite often, pushing himself with determination around the corridors in his wheelchair (or latterly being pushed), because he could not bear to be alone in his room. When I looked at his face I saw a blank expression, but behind this I think I glimpsed fear. He seemed to need to keep moving, always pushing himself forward, in order to remain one step ahead of the fear. And when he was in his room he would listen to his music, his headphones keeping the world at bay. I wanted to speak with him, to offer to share a tiny bit of the journey with him, but he did not give me the chance. I felt helpless in the presence of his fear, and frustrated that I could do nothing. And, of course, what I felt mirrored the experience of his parents and sisters.

One day in the hospice I went into the room of a woman who was living with motor neurone disease. I knew her quite well and we had a good rapport. But on this particular day I was feeling tired and not very patient. Because of the terrible loss of control that the disease brings, she needed to have everything around her in exactly the right place. I noticed that she had her Litewriter® – a wonderful communication device for those with little mobility that spells out words letter by letter – on the side table and a tea towel folded up on her lap. When I had said 'Hallo' she moved her head slightly, indicating that she wanted me to do something for her. I was not sure what she needed. First I tried moving the Litewriter on to her lap. She moved her head more insistently. Her hand moved ever so slightly to the tea towel and her eyes focused on it. I suddenly realized that she wanted me to wipe her mouth with the tea towel. I did this, and moved the Litewriter back to the table. She moved her hand again, ever so slightly. I wondered if she wanted the control for her chair, so I placed the control nearer to her hand. She was beginning now to become distressed. I tried placing the Litewriter back on her lap, but it was not in the right position for her. I moved it several times before it was in exactly the right position so that she could operate it. After 20 minutes in her presence I felt worn out, useless and quite angry with her for 'making me' feel useless. And, of course, this woman was teaching me something very important: she was showing me how infuriating it was for her to be trapped in a body that barely worked, and how angry and distressed she became when she could not communicate her most basic needs to others.

The frustration and anger in these encounters reveal my desire to 'fix' people. I have been aware of this impulse in myself for many, many years. I want to make things better. I want to take away distress. What is the meaning of this deep desire? For me the sequence is like this: I feel helpless and useless; this is intolerable; instead of staying with the helplessness I will grasp back control and try to make things change. The desire to *fix it* is a defence against helplessness.

Swallows

My family and I were staying for a week in a Christian community called Othona, near Bradwell-on-Sea in Essex. The first morning I woke early and decided to walk up to what we call 'the chapel'. This is St Peter-on-the-Wall, and it claims to be the oldest church in the country still in use. St Cedd founded a monastery here in the sixth century, recycling the Roman brick from the abandoned fort of Othona. And although the chapel was used as a barn for many years, it has been restored and is a sacred place once more. Prayer is in its walls. When I walked in that morning I was immediately aware of swallows chattering in the rafters. I had noticed them on the previous evening during the chapel service. My intention had been to find some stillness and to pray, but I was concerned for the trapped swallows. I therefore opened the great wooden door to allow them to fly out. They were crying plaintively to one another, flying back and forth, flapping at the high windows. At last one spiralled down and flew out of the door into the open air. My heart leapt for joy. And after a further wait a second swallow flew out. But then another bird flew straight in, and it was not a swallow! It hurled itself against the windows again and again, trying to escape from the confined space. Now I felt guilty that I had left the door open. When I eventually left I closed the door behind me for fear of other birds flying in, and I walked back to the camp feeling I had failed in my mission of rescuing the birds. Instead of finding stillness I had found anxiety.

The following morning, when everyone had arrived for chapel, the door was left open and the swallows simply swooped out one after the other. There was no sign of the other visitor – perhaps it had found its way out through an opening under the eaves. During the week the birds came and went according to their own desires, and I relaxed about their well-being. As I reflected on this I realized that I was trying to control the behaviour of the swallows, and by my anxious intervention I potentially made the situation worse. The swallows did not need my assistance; they could fix the problem for themselves. I further realized that during this community week I was not feeling in control. I had a very small part to play in leading the week as my wife and son were doing the bulk of it; I needed to trust them and the process of the week. The swallows were revealing my anxious need to be in control.

Crucified

I find it hard to be with the story of the crucifixion of Christ in an imaginative way. It is natural to avoid suffering that we cannot do anything about, but those of us who try to care for the dying and their families need to be able to face the suffering we cannot fix. I read the account of the crucifixion in Mark 15.21–41.

> I see Simon carrying the crosspiece. 'Go Simon, go!' chant the crowd mockingly; they point and they jeer. I scuttle around in between people, a small being in the midst of a great crowd, trying to see what is happening, wanting to do something but feeling ineffectual. They want Jesus to have a sedative and I want to encourage him to take some pain relief. But he refuses. And they hammer the nails in and hoist him up. I am at a distance with the women. At one point, taking my courage in my hands, I come over to the soldiers and ask them, 'Why do you need to do this? Why do you need to kill?' They laugh at one another. 'There's someone here who wants a revolution, Fred! We can always get another cross for you, Sonny.' And they push me back to where the women are standing. It gets dark. I look at these

women who have cared for Jesus throughout his ministry. 'How do you do this?' I ask. 'How do you stay here?' One of them looks at me through her tears, 'It's what you have to do, isn't it? It's just what you do.' I cannot comfort them. I cannot alter what is happening. I cannot make a difference. The cry of desolation is terrible. 'My God, my God, why have you forsaken me?' And the mocking is terrible. I cannot stop his dying.

In the hospice a mother cannot stop the dying for her daughter; a husband cannot stop the dying for his wife; a grandson cannot stop the dying for his grandfather. The pain of this is beyond words.

I must be able to do something. They must be able to do something. You must be able to do something.

Of course, there are some things that we can do. There is pain relief, bowel care, massage, reflexology, kind volunteers, creative therapies, listening to the story, presence. But the one thing we cannot fix is the dying. It will happen – perhaps not exactly when we expect, but death is inevitable. Sometimes, with great love and courage, words of release are spoken to a loved one.

It's OK, Derek . . . It's OK, Jan . . . It's OK, Paul . . . It's OK, Mary . . . you can let go now.

Words of release, which may help the person on their journey.

We can't stop this. We love you, and we let you go.

Losing control

I can feel anxious because of the loss of control that inevitably goes with the dying process. This part of my self needs to be listened to (Loss of Control – L):

B   Hallo.

L   I'm surprised you want to talk to me.

B   Are you. Why's that?

L   Because I scare you.

B   Ahh . . .

L   I am the date for going back to school that you feared so much, the hospital appointment you couldn't avoid, the exam you had to take, the breath you could not catch. You fear me because you cannot change me.

B   I fear you because you make bad things happen to me.

L   That's not true. You fear me because you like to be master of your own destiny, and I won't let you. Where I go you go.

B   I do hate you for that. I hate the feeling of having to do things when you want me to do them. I hate the idea that I could die at any moment and there is nothing I could do to stop it. I don't like being thwarted in my desires and my plans – and you thwart me all the time. You make me dance to your tune. You let me believe that I am sorting out my life, and then you lob another hand grenade into my soul. Thank you so much!

L   I'm your friend, Bob.

B   How do you work that out?

L   I teach you to be less dependent on your own wishes and desires.

B   What's wrong with my wishes and desires?

L   I teach you to trust the only one who may be trusted.

B   Ahh . . .

L   I am the soft rain that falls unbidden from the sky to refresh your tired face. I am the wind that blows you into the good future that is not of your own

making. I am the laughter that erupts from your
soul when you see grace at work in the essence of
things.

B   OK, OK ...

L   I am your death – yes I know how you hate me for
that. I will carry you through the door when the time
is right. And then you will be pierced by love.

B   Perhaps I can learn to accept what I cannot change.
I think that might be a definition of maturity. I don't
want to keep on trying to control and fix everything.
I limit the possibilities when I try to do that – close
it all down.

L   I will open it all up for you.

B   Hmm ...

This reflection yields important information. The loss of
control is experienced keenly by my childself. He needs loving in the fears surrounding what cannot be changed for
him. But he also asks to be heard in the experience of being
'thwarted'; when he cannot have his own way this is very
painful for him. Finally, the emergent self is beginning to
see the potential in letting go of control.

Learning to trust

Let us return to the account of my abortive attempt to give
freedom to the swallows. During that week I needed to trust
my co-leaders, who were far more experienced than I in
the work we were doing. I needed to lean on them and let
them do most of the work. I find it hard to trust when I feel
anxious and helpless; it takes courage to trust when everything seems up in the air. How can I find that courage?

When I am with a person who is dying, and their distressed
family who wait in helplessness at the bedside, I am receiving an invitation to trust. In the face of something that

nobody can change I can trust that God is present. He is present in the terrible facts of the situation. Recognized or unrecognized, he is there in the realities of what is going on. The resources of faith can be useful, and they are to be used. Scripture, song, Holy Communion, the anointing with oil, prayer, silence – all of these can be very helpful. Their use suggests, 'Something more is going on here than meets the eye.'

A hospice is a cross-shaped institution because at its heart is a compassion in which suffering is not taken away but held as well as we can hold it. It is of course easy to romanticize the cross and forget that for Christ the cross meant a bloody and terrifying ordeal. I am suspicious when someone tells me, 'Simply trust in God and all will turn out well.' All may not turn out well. The death of a loved one can feel absolutely and irrevocably wrong. So perhaps the trust we need is that even the despair can somehow be held. The container that is the hospice is bigger than me and bigger than any one of us. We cannot stop the dying but it will be as good as it can be. When the dying comes it is often nothing like as terrifying as people expect (although sometimes it is of course). It is the waiting that is so hard – waiting in love, wishing it were all over and feeling guilty that you wish it were all over. Our task is to wait with those who are waiting.

So I can find the courage to trust. I can trust 'hospice' which, more than just the actual place, is also a spiritual reality. People often say, 'This is such a peaceful place', and I am surprised, knowing the stresses that live just under the surface. But yes, there is peace; I can trust the peace. And I can trust myself a little more. I will listen carefully, put some words into a prayer, hold a hand or touch someone's arm. I cannot fix it but I can be there. Perhaps that is enough. Sometimes it feels enough; sometimes it feels like being in the right place at the right time.

And I can trust the process of dying. Sleep is very healing; a baby sleeps through much of her early life, and we usually sleep a lot at the end of our lives. When we are dying we relinquish our desires. First of all we let go of our desire for food; then water; finally air. Pain relief makes a vast difference. Sometimes it is not a perfect death but it is often a good-enough one – and death can sometimes be amazingly beautiful. There can be a sense of joy – of a person having journeyed on. And although the dead body is to be treated with great reverence and love, this physical entity seems no longer to be the true person; there is a qualitative difference. I can learn to trust all these things.

13
It is as it is

A bicycle ride

I was cycling home, feeling dissatisfied with myself. This was not a very strong reaction, but rather a dull, background feeling of discontent. As I pushed wearily on the pedals I felt I had not 'done' enough that day. In my mind I went over one particular conversation with a patient and her husband that I thought had not gone very well. I realized that I had been wanting them to find peace and acceptance in the awfulness of their experience, in order that I could feel better about their situation. I felt that during the whole day I had not been as authentic as I could have been. I was trying to 'perform' in the interactions rather than let the conversations flow.

And as I cycled I suddenly thought, 'It is as it is.' This was a consoling thought, which I later took into my praying. I discovered that 'It is as it is' can be a helpful mantra. The day has been as it has been, and my conversations and reactions have been as they have been. Myself, and the people I have met, have been as we have been at this particular moment in our histories. I cannot change any of it. I can reflect on it and my reactions to it but the imperfect day will not change through my being dissatisfied with it – and that is fine!

What lies behind the dissatisfaction I have described? As I reflected, I found a familiar inner landscape emerging:

In my imagination, somewhere over there, just out of reach, is a perfect state of being where I should be.

Others have found it but I am stumbling around 'here' in the boggy ground in my wellies. Sometimes I find solid ground but I know that very soon the solid ground will give way to bog again. I can never quite reach this perfect place but I know I should be there.

The word 'should' of course is very significant. It implies some internal or external pressure. I also know that understanding the 'should' is the way to being comfortable in the less-than-perfect place with my less-than-perfect self. This is the only place we can sit as people who attempt to care for others.

Perfectionism

Perfectionism is rife in the Church. It means keeping the rules, living up to the expectations, achieving a quality of life that will please God. There is a huge pressure here, and good Christian people can drive themselves remorselessly to be the sort of person God will approve of. The problem is, they will never be that person. I think of a church many years ago that welcomed a friend of ours who was an alcoholic. They nurtured him well while he was not drinking. When he went back to the bottle they withdrew their care and support. Perfectionism is very unloving. When we want everyone to achieve the right moral standards we do not truly love the other person, because we have conditions that must be met. Neither do we love ourselves.

As a young Methodist minister I put myself under great pressure to live up to God's standards and the standards of the Church. I set myself up to be a saint and spent much time struggling with prayer – not because I was delighting in God's presence but because I wished to attain holiness. I preached energetic sermons and attempted to impress everyone with my tireless visiting of the flock. But all the time

I knew there was a huge gap between the person I wanted to be and the person I knew myself to be. It is very foolish to try to be a saint in one's own efforts, and inevitably I slipped up on the banana skin that was uniquely mine to slip on. In my fall I discovered the joy of being human rather than perfect.

The whole basis of perfectionism is 'You've got to change.' The person we are now is not acceptable and a new person must be born. The sinful aspects of the self must be hacked away in order for this new person to come into being. In Christianity the clear message is that this cannot happen through our own efforts but only through the grace of God. However, the way we live often gives the lie to this. We strive for this ideal and screw up our energies to be a different person. All of this effort is totally barren.

Wholeness is very different from perfectionism. I think of wholeness as a large circle in which all our imperfections reside. They cease to have so much power over us and are manageable precisely because they are held in the circle that is the good self. This circle in turn is contained within the greater circle of God's love. I can love myself with this thought.

Let things be different

In the hospice I sense a great desire for things to be different – this is absolutely natural. I sense it in patients, relatives, volunteers and staff. One of our doctors once said to me jokingly, 'Bob, can't you make it all better?' If only things were different. Sometimes I listen as a patient tells me that, despite all evidence to the contrary, their cancer has gone away. Occasionally I am asked to pray for a miracle so that a loved one will not die. Often I hear the unspoken cry of the heart that longs to be healthy and in control of life again. And I hear the silent scream of a relative, desperately trying to hold on to their loved one as they used to be before the disease process began.

Karen Murphy, a hospice chaplain in Weston-super-Mare, asked a volunteer who was a talented artist to paint four pictures of a river. The first picture shows a stream that is young and turbulent. In the next, the river has straightened out and there is a calm, except for a heron on the bank – an ambivalent image. There is another picture of the river with a large boulder in the middle of it, and the last is of a beautiful lake with the sun either setting or rising. The images can represent different stages of the inner journey with a life-limiting disease. The chaplain asks patients to choose the picture that rings true for them, and encourages them to paint a picture of their own journey, as a river. The exercise invites people to say something like, 'This is how it is. I know that I am dying and this is what it is like. This is how it is at this particular stage of the journey. This is where the river has taken me thus far.' Note that this is a playful, indirect way of expressing huge pain.

Stones into bread

I tried an interesting prayer exercise that focuses on our desire for change and perfection. In the temptations of Christ, the Tempter urges him to change stones into bread (Luke 4.1–13). After fasting for 40 days (a biblical term for a long period of time, not literally 40 days), preparing himself for the work ahead, he was hungry. Why not use his God-given powers to turn the rocks of the wilderness into bread? He could satisfy his hunger, and if this seemed a little self-serving he could feed the hungry of the land while he was at it. His refusal to do so speaks powerfully to me of the need to accept reality as it is. His hunger is real and is part of the experience of spiritual preparation. It is not to be magicked away – 'It is as it is'. It is hard to be in the wilderness – as hard as rock. I wondered if I could try turning stones into 'bread'. What might that reveal?

I took a reasonably large stone with sharp edges and sat holding it. In my mind I formed the words, 'Let this stone become . . .'. I tried out some fairly wild fantasies that did not take me anywhere. Then I tried a little alchemy and said to myself, 'Let this stone become gold.' I thought of a golden paten and chalice – there was absolutely no life in the imagining. I also tried, 'Let this stone become a bird.' I imagined the freedom of flying but there was no life here either.

Eventually I thought of the stone remaining itself, but now it was in community with other stones. I thought of my stone becoming part of a labyrinth and I imagined my stone incorporated into a cathedral. Then I saw it held securely in the wall of the ancient church of St Peter-on-the-Wall, Bradwell, which I know so well (and which we visited in the last chapter of course). These latter thoughts gave me great consolation and peace. By now the stone was quite warm, which interested me. I thought of being held in the warmth and love of God. The stone had stayed very stone-like throughout the exercise. It did not lose its roughness, it did not change into something else; but it could be warmed and it could be placed alongside other stones.

Sitting with the other person

When I am listening to someone I sometimes have a great need to get it 'right'. I *must* respond genuinely, compassionately, spiritually and 'appropriately'. I must not make a 'mistake' in this delicate process. I must be warm but not too friendly. I must keep the boundaries but be compassionate. I must ask gentle, open questions designed to take the person to a deeper level of conversation but I must never be intrusive. I must of course be praying all the time I am with the person but I must not impose my spirituality on them. When there is a silence it must be comfortable for both parties.

Furthermore, by my perfect spiritual intervention, my fantasy is that I will effect a change in the other person. They will become more peaceful, less anxious, more able to face their dying, more comfortable with their past, more accepting of those they have alienated in this life. I, the perfect carer, must make this happen. I exaggerate of course, but the expectations we have of ourselves float under the surface of our consciousness, revealing themselves in reactions such as dissatisfaction. Or we may overreact to criticism. Our internal reaction may be, 'How dare you prick the bubble of my perfectionism and expose the reality of how it is!'

What I have described is the perfect listening encounter – and this perfect encounter can never be. It is an ideal, and the ideal can so often be the enemy of the actual. I can do nothing to change another human being (the only person I can change, by grace, is myself). What a glorious freedom there is here in this realization!

I believe the invitation for us is to sit with another person with the full awareness of our imperfections. This in itself is helpful to the other person. They will pick this up from us under the surface of the conversation. It will give them the freedom to be imperfect too. They will not have to try to give us anything, as though they owe us something for coming to see them. They will not try to pretend to be in a different place from the actual place they inhabit right now. They will simply be where they are, the person they are, with their desolation, their longings and their goodness. I am who I am in the glory of my imperfection; you are who you are in the glory of your imperfection. Then something remarkable can happen: the Perfect One, however we name him or her, can be in the space between us. There can be an honesty and genuine peace in the words or the silence.

Nobody is trying; we are simply allowing the Spirit to be, and wondering at the beauty of it.

There is, of course, a danger here also. This desire for the future, for change, for the perfect is so strong in many of us that we may be disappointed when we do not experience this 'glory of imperfection'. The temptation is to try to make this 'letting it be as it is' happen! I think we are invited to cultivate the attitude of letting be in our times of contemplation and reflection. But old habits die hard – this is a lifelong task. We need to be very gentle with ourselves.

The garden

When we came to Oxford we bought a house that needed a lot of work doing to it. Four years down the road we are still trying to improve things. Of course, C. G. Jung might remind me that a house can be a symbol of the self. I referred to some of the inhabitants of our garden in the first chapter. One day I sat on the new patio looking out over the unfinished garden and thought:

> The garden is as it is; the pine cabin with the disturbing gaps between the planks, caused by we know not what; the herb garden made from recycled concrete blocks, still ugly until the plants grow over the edges; the pile of earth on top of the blue tarpaulin; the lawn with its molehills and natural undulations. It is all exactly as it is. Imperfect, but glorious in the June sunshine. And if I can accept it just as it is, then – paradoxically – change is possible.

If I can accept myself as I am, as an imperfect but glorious carer for others, then growth is possible. I think there is a discipline of thanksgiving that helps us here. We may give thanks for the actuality of our relationships, our work, our situation in life – and this gradually changes us.

14

Grateful

Giving thanks

Some people, when they are dying (and it is often those who have lived a reasonably long life), can arrive at a place of deep gratitude. A person might be experiencing some anxiety and pain, but in the hospice small things can have great meaning. A robin flies to the bird-table and pecks at the seed; a friend comes to visit and brings in the latest news from the outside world; a cup of tea and a piece of cake are shared (made in the hospice kitchen so that it tastes like home cooking); a blackbird taps at the glass door of the room; sudden, vivid memories from childhood come flooding back; family come to visit and bring with them a great-grandchild's extravagant, bold painting; a card arrives from a relative in New Zealand. These simple gifts are savoured, turned over in the mind and enjoyed to the full. I hear the heartfelt gratitude for a son or a daughter who has cared beyond the normal bounds of duty, and I hear gratitude for the kindness of hospice staff and volunteers. This person has come to terms with her appointment with death, but still finds joy in living. She enjoys her bath – complete with bubbles; she enjoys talking to the healthcare assistant about her family; she enjoys a Baileys from the drinks trolley before supper.

Giving out of our gift

Jesus entered Jericho and was passing through. A man was there by the name of Zacchaeus; he was a chief tax collector and was wealthy. He wanted to see who Jesus was, but being a short man he could not, because of the crowd. So he ran ahead and climbed a sycamore-fig tree to see him, since Jesus was coming that way. When Jesus reached the spot, he looked up and said to him, 'Zacchaeus, come down immediately. I must stay at your house today.' So he came down at once and welcomed him gladly. All the people saw this and began to mutter, 'He has gone to be the guest of a "sinner".' But Zacchaeus stood up and said to the Lord, 'Look, Lord! Here and now I give half of my possessions to the poor, and if I have cheated anybody out of anything, I will pay back four times the amount.' Jesus said to him, 'Today salvation has come to this house, because this man, too, is a son of Abraham. For the Son of Man came to seek and to save what was lost.'

(Luke 19.1–10)

Whenever I visualize this passage I see Zacchaeus on the pavement outside of his house, giving away his money. He has a big grin on his face and although he knows some people are coming round twice, he does not care a fig. Here is the archetypal enemy – a taxman and fellow countryman in the employ of the occupying forces; a man who has become ridiculously rich because he has the protection of the enemy. But the hated Zacchaeus has received something greater than money: he has discovered he can belong again. He is no longer a man on the outside looking in, but a true son of Abraham. His gratitude knows no bounds.

We cannot give until we have first received. Zacchaeus would not be out there on the pavement giving away his money had he not first received. And so it is for those of us who try to care for others – we give out of our gift.

Cultivating a habit of gratitude is something I know I need to work on. Let me list some of the things I can be thankful for in my pastoral work:

- *The moment in time when I am fully present to another person.* There may not be many such moments if I am honest, because I easily live in the past or the future. But when I am truly in the here and now, I know it – and I give thanks for what happens in the space between myself and that other person.

- *The growing of a listening relationship over a period of time.* This happens in our day-care unit and sometimes on the ward. I get to know someone and the trust begins to grow. I stay with the person's concerns, whatever they may be. I come back, again and again. Something deepens.

- *The pastoral-care team in the hospice.* I am so fortunate in being surrounded by compassionate, curious and supportive people. I cannot do this work by myself – it is too big – and I am learning to rejoice when another person in the team is able to support a patient when I have not been able to. A while back I went on my own to talk about spiritual care to a group of people I did not know. I made myself very vulnerable in what I said to them, and felt misunderstood. After that hard evening, when I am now asked to talk about the work of the hospice I always try to go with at least one other member of the team. The experience is very different because I am speaking from a place of community. I also give thanks for my chaplaincy colleagues – particularly for the gift of honesty about the struggles we have with the work.

- *Listening to staff.* Those who come to work in a hospice do so for many different reasons, and I have certainly wondered why I am here. I suspect many of us are trying to come to terms with our wounds or our mortality. Staff and patients *seem* to inhabit two different worlds. The one group has the role of active carer, the other of passive patient. But the staff are also patients, in that we have our own wounded inner selves to care for. I am grateful for the times when a member of staff is able to talk honestly to me about the challenges he or she is facing.

- *Recovery time after a period of intense work.* I sometimes have a run of days full of challenging encounters. I am drained of energy, but then follows some time away from the hospice. I take the dogs for a long walk in the woods, have a luxurious bath, complete with coffee, cake and book. I write, reflect and play the piano. My soul comes alive again and I give thanks.

In the modern practice of Ignatian spirituality, gratitude is of fundamental importance. At the end of the day – or in the morning, looking back over the previous day – I sometimes ask myself two questions: 'What am I most grateful for about today?' and 'What am I least grateful for?' Whenever I do this I find it helpful – I can relive the life-giving times in my imagination, which is very strengthening because otherwise I overemphasize the negatives and underemphasize the positives for which I *can* give thanks.

When the universe turns against you

We cannot always give thanks, so let us look at what gets in the way. Sometimes when people are dying, nothing is 'right'. How can it be right for a mother to die when her role is to care for and protect her young children? How can it be right for a man to die when he has only been married to his young wife for a year? How can it be right for the body to turn against you and become an enemy instead of a friend? There is a profound sense of the disease process being unfair. It feels personal, as though you have been singled out for punishment. At first I was surprised by how many people in the hospice talked to me in terms of doing something wrong and being punished by God. The idea of a vengeful God still lingers in the collective unconscious and is one of the most unhelpful aspects of religion. But the theory is perfectly understandable, for we are meaning-makers and will find any way of making sense of things, however crazy. After all, if your body is failing you and paining you, it *feels* like punishment. You need to blame someone or something so you blame God, the doctors or life itself: 'It is not meant to be like this; it is just not fair.' As I was cycling to work one day in winter I watched a mother walking along the pavement with her toddler. Suddenly the little girl slipped and fell into an icy puddle. She yelled, and the yell expressed outrage that the universe could behave in such a way towards her. Those who are dying may 'yell' in a similar way. It is the helplessness that is so hard. Your body turns on you; you can no longer *do*. On the whole we do not make the transition from *doing* to *being* without much suffering.

Our cultural context

One way to understand a culture is to look at its television adverts. The advertising industry in this country is death-denying. We have been drip-fed the story that we will stay young, sexy, strong and successful for ever. A consumer society needs its consumers to stay alive and consuming, so dying is not part of the deal. No wonder we get a shock when death is there staring us in the face – we have simply not been prepared.

Neither does our culture encourage gratitude. It is my right to have things – to have happiness, work, material prosperity, health and fulfilling relationships. I don't have to thank somebody for what is mine by right. When I say 'Thank you' I am making myself vulnerable – putting myself at your mercy. The fear underneath the surface is that if these things have been given then they may also be taken away. If I think they are mine by right I can maintain the fantasy that I can have them for ever.

Unfair

There are times when I feel life is not fair. 'Unfair' is the opposite of 'Thank you'. I hate this feeling but I can all too easily drop into it. It is not fair that I am so tired. It is not fair that I am doing so much. I compare myself with others close to me and compete with them to see who is the most hard-done-by! This hard-done-by self feels that no one cares for him or listens to him; he is full of self-pity. The challenge is to move from griping to gratitude. Here the Hard-done-by Self (H) is in full spate:

H   I am so FRUSTRATED!

B   Why?

H   I thought I was going to do a funeral for a patient and they are messing me around.

B   Who is?

H   The family. They are going for a service in an Anglican church now and it's just getting so COMPLICATED. The local vicar is going to do the service and he's asked me to do A SHORT ADDRESS and it's miles away. I thought I would be doing THE WHOLE THING at the Crematorium. I'm going to need to arrange to have the car that day. And they don't really need two clergy-people doing the service. It's a WASTE OF TIME – I could be getting on with other things here. I just DON'T want to do it.

B   You sound like a little boy who isn't getting his own way. Your little kingdom isn't being established as you want. You're not in control of this are you? Someone else has taken over and you don't like it. You're not getting the glory.

H   No I DON'T like it.

B   Aha . . .

H   They're not giving me centre stage . . .

B   What's good about having centre stage?

H I'm important if I have centre stage. People give me recognition.

B And what's not so good about having centre stage?

H If I get it wrong then I will look stupid.

B This is important stuff isn't it?

H I know it doesn't get me anywhere though.

B So what might get you somewhere?

H To let go of the glory. To accept that something good might happen in a situation where I am not in charge. And to see it from the family's point of view perhaps. There are conflicts in the family and that's why we've ended up with something different for the funeral. They're not deliberately trying to make life difficult for me.

B And to give thanks for the life of Sarah?

H Yes, I was forgetting that. To give thanks for her. She might even pray for me if I'm lucky.

Having reacted in this way, and by allowing myself to *feel* the powerful, affronted feelings, I was able to take part in the service happily without the feelings intruding into the external world of the funeral.

Giving thanks with the whole of my self

Psalm 103 begins with these words: 'Praise the LORD, O my soul; all my inmost being, praise his holy name.' This made me think about giving thanks with everything in my inmost being. I wondered if I could really give thanks out of the more 'difficult' selves in my community of the self. Could I glimpse some possibility of transformation through gratitude? I looked at a vase of daffodils and this is the journey of my imagination:

I give thanks for these flowers,
For the colour yellow;
They shine like the sun.

My hard-done-by self says, 'They are too fine for me,
They dance in the light,
They are too full of life.
I should have dandelions, not daffodils.'
And he takes the vase away and puts it in the cupboard.
Then he goes outside looking for
Something less ostentatious,
Less exuberant.
But he can't find any dandelions.
All he can find is a sunflower
Growing in the grass verge
Between the pavement and the road.
And he looks at this flower
In wonder.

My fearful self says, 'There will be no more daffodils,
They are trampled in the mud
By heavy boots,
By marching boots,
Their beauty gone for ever.'
But Fear goes into the mud,
Picks them out,
Takes them home,
Washes and dries them,
Then weaves them into a hanging sculpture.
They are beautiful.

My shameful self says, 'I have done wrong,
I have taken these flowers from the Queen's garden
And they were not mine to take.
They do not shine,
They are full of death.'
So Shame goes in fear and trembling to the Queen
and finds her walking alone in the garden.
'I have stolen from you,' he says, his head down, face
    red.

She smiles gently and says, 'But this is our garden, not
   mine!
Take another bunch;
Have as many bunches as you can carry.'

My proud self says, 'I have made these.
By my own will and power
I have created daffodils.
Look at them in awe.
Look on my power.'
But Pride was clumsy, and as he threw
His arms about, demonstrating his skill,
He knocked the vase off its shelf.
It fell to the floor
And smashed.
Pride looked at the mess,
Got down on his knees
And carefully collected up the flowers.
He went next door
And shyly gave them to the elderly couple
Who live there.

In our listening work perhaps we can learn to turn things
around in a similar way to this reflection. When we acknowledge and befriend the shadow selves we harness their power
and they can work for us instead of against us. After all, there
is a huge amount of energy tied up in these selves. By facing
the shadow selves, listening to them and loving them, they
may actually turn into their opposites. The acknowledged
fear of illness and dying lends its energy to courage; the
acknowledged shame lends its energy to loving and desiring
the growth of another person; the acknowledged proud,
unyielding self lends its energy to the joy of letting go. When
I can give thanks for these shadow selves, for the whole of
me, I may sit and listen to a person and they no longer hijack
the process – they actually *energize* it. The community of the

self sings out in love and gratitude and the shadow selves weave their unique melodies into the song.

The funeral as gratitude

The final word here is about funerals. There has been a movement in the last few decades towards the funeral becoming a celebration of a person's life. As our society has become more secularized the focus of the service has changed. A funeral service used to be a service in which God was worshipped, and in that context of praise a person's life was remembered. Now the focus is on celebrating a human life while perhaps adding in some spiritual or religious material. I do not bemoan this at all. To me God is present whether named or unnamed. The good thing is that a family these days has much more control over the content of the service – the officiant is like a master of ceremonies, holding everything together (and hoping that the ceremony will not overrun!). Tributes are given by members of the family, colleagues or friends, and these costly, personal speeches enable the whole congregation to cherish the person who has died. Funny stories make people laugh – and most people are relieved to be able to laugh, for the atmosphere can, of course, be heavy. Memories flow through the mind; music evokes special times shared together; loss and gratitude are experienced at the same time. For the closest relatives there may be a feeling of unreality about the whole event. Numbness is all that they feel; and the burden of organizing and attending a big service can be huge. Even so there can be gratitude that family, friends and colleagues have come together to remember. The service in church or at the crematorium is usually followed by refreshments of some sort, providing everyone with a further opportunity to tell stories about the person who has died and to let death return again to the far corner of the mind where it normally resides. The day of the funeral can truly be a day of gratitude.

15

The place just right

In 1848, Elder Joseph Brackett wrote a song for his Shaker community of Alfred, Maine, in the United States. He called it 'Simple Gifts' (Sydney Carter later adapted the tune for his song 'Lord of the Dance'), and here are the words:

'Tis the gift to be simple, 'tis the gift to be free,
'Tis the gift to come down where we ought to be,
And when we find ourselves in the place just right,
'Twill be in the valley of love and delight.
When true simplicity is gain'd,
To bow and to bend we shan't be asham'd,
To turn, turn will be our delight,
'Til by turning, turning we come round right.

The words, 'when we find ourselves in the place just right', can describe the experience of a listening encounter that simply flows. There can be tremendous joy – even in the middle of distress and sadness – when we lose concern for ourselves and sink into an engagement with another person in the timeless present. And here we are at the heart of soul reflection: through the reflective process we are freed up to be of use to the person we are listening to. By finding the right place ourselves, we will be inviting them into it as well.

Gift

When I was at sixth-form college many years ago we were encouraged to engage in some kind of voluntary work; for a time I used to visit a centre for adults with profound physical and mental disabilities. This was the first time I had encountered people who were so very different from myself, and I used to dread my visits. I was self-conscious and awkward and did not know how to relate to the people there. But there was one occasion when I made a visit, and all of the anxiety simply disappeared. I was suddenly able to see through the disabilities and recognize the real, beautiful people who were not so different from myself after all. My heart was filled with the gift of compassion, the separateness melted away and I saw that all of us were loved equally by the same mystery we name God. We cannot make this happen – it is pure gift. All we can do is rejoice when we find that we are there in that right place with the right person at the right time.

Balance

The 'place just right' is not a place where there is an absence of internal conflict – that place will never exist. Rather it is a place where darkness and light, fear and joy, sadness and hope are held together in something greater than ourselves. I have found that the reflective process *itself* is this right place. When we honestly explore the terrain of our inner world, playing with our reactions, allowing our different selves to speak to us through the imagination, then we are on solid ground. We discover a kind of balance.

There is a story that C. G. Jung heard from a man called Richard Wilhelm, who had been living in a part of China experiencing a severe drought. Stories change as they are transmitted, and this is my version:

It had not rained for such a long time that the crops were failing and the cattle were dying. People were becoming concerned for their survival. So the King called for his magicians and priests and ordered them to bring the rain. They made spells, performed rituals and recited prayers, but there was no rain. In desperation he sent for the Rainmaker, who lived in a neighbouring kingdom up in the mountains. When he arrived at the court some days later, the Rainmaker turned out to be a bent, insignificant-looking old man. The King asked what he needed to make the rain come. All he requested was a hut in the valley and solitude. The King's courtiers quickly found a simple shepherd's hut for him and left the Rainmaker to his work. Four days later the rain came and the people danced for joy in the puddles. The King called the Rainmaker back to the court and he was showered with presents. Eventually the King asked him how he managed to achieve such an amazing feat when everyone else had failed. 'Well,' said the Rainmaker, 'in my country everything is in balance. When I entered your kingdom I immediately realized that everything was out of balance, and this affected me deeply. For three days I sat in silence in order to find my true centre. And when my internal balance was restored on the fourth day, it rained, because the balance of the country was also restored.'

(Wilhelm said that what he reported really did happen, though in his version the rain was followed by snow, unheard of at that time of year.)

The Rainmaker's solitude is at the centre of this story, and I know that my listening work flows best out of my emptiness and stillness. I need times in the year when I go away to be with silence and find renewal in my innermost being. I need times in each day when I can allow the clamouring voices in my head to be heard, and welcome in the energy and peace of God. In stillness I find my balance. I am then less likely to get in the way as the person I am listening to tries to find more balance in *their* living.

A beautiful image comes from the Spiritual Exercises of Ignatius of Loyola: 'Therefore, the director of the Exercises, as a balance at equilibrium, without leaning to one side or the other, should permit the Creator to deal directly with the creature, and the creature directly with his Creator and Lord.'[1]

When I am balanced I am not concerned about 'getting it right' or what impression I am making on the people around me. I find I wish to get it 'real' rather than 'right'. I want to let God be God. No longer pulled away by fear, I am free to be with another person, without trying to change them. I am simply myself, with empty hands and empty heart – and the space between us seems to sparkle with love and compassion.

Another way of looking at balance is in terms of the relationship between our different selves. When I practise the art of reflection I make room for the selves I am not so comfortable with. I welcome in the shameful self, the angry self and the fearful self. They come in from the cold and become part of the internal community once more. Before this happened, the greater self was skewed and off-centre; now it comes right. The self has a balanced 'feel' to it; it is at peace with itself, comfortable, like a dog in winter stretched out in front of the fire.

Ego

The place just right is the space where ego – in its popular sense rather than as, more technically, our centre of consciousness – is held in God's love. I don't think we should ever try to get rid of ego – it is a powerhouse containing so much good elemental energy. Think of the toddler, banging her head on the hard floor because she has been stopped from pulling the dog's tail. Here is such will, such power that can be transformed into creative, loving action as she grows older. The ego is not bad; it is just raw, unchannelled energy wanting its own ends, intent on its own survival. Ego is unhelpful to us when it is left unattended; then it will always try to be God. What ego needs so desperately is to be lovingly embraced and then allowed to splash and play at the real God's seaside.

'Simple Gifts' refers to bowing, bending and turning. In an age when we are encouraged to stand up for our rights and be assertive this sounds like unhealthy subservience. But perhaps the words indicate a way of service and of freedom where ego is no longer in control. I have developed a strange ritual with one of our Czech housekeepers. When I come into the hospice in the morning we bow in mock seriousness three times and then laugh at each other. Underneath the joke we are expressing respect and liking for one another. In the same way, when we really listen to another person our heart is bowing in respect to their uniqueness. Our ego bends its shape so that we can be receptive to their identity, fears, hopes and desire. Perhaps this is yet another way of understanding reflective practice. We turn so that we can see from a different angle, and in turning may glimpse a beautiful soul. Through bowing, bending and turning, the song suggests, we 'come round right'.

When I am with someone who is dying, ego often falls obediently into his rightful place. It is as though he knows instinctively that this is not the time to try to grab attention or to look clever. Instead ego just sits there quietly like a dog waiting at his master's feet. He lends his energy, because that is needed in any challenging situation; he allows the soul to make the connection and does not get in the way. Then two human beings may discover the simplicity of communicating at a profound level, in the silence, through touch or with words.

A right place beyond words

I find that I get frustrated with words. They are needful but they miss the mark too often. I like time to sculpt my sentences but in the middle of a highly charged conversation I do not have the luxury of time; I respond in the moment and sometimes my speech feels unnatural and forced. Some people cannot say anything back to me because of their physical state, so I need to be aware that a conversation may actually be an awkward monologue on my part. And in the face of huge anguish and unbearable suffering, there are just no words to say. Perhaps we are hearing an invitation to go beyond words.

There is a saying, 'The eyes are the windows of the soul.' We talk about the importance of eye-contact but perhaps eye-contact can become soul-contact. Eastern religions talk about the importance of 'soft eyes'. What is being communicated as I hold the gaze of a patient or relative for a few moments in the silence? It may be something like this:

> You are OK. Ultimately you are safe and whole in spite of all the evidence to the contrary. I am with you in this moment. My soul is open to you. I have not much strength myself, so perhaps together we can reach out to the One in whom we live and move and have our being.

Occasionally I will sing or hum quietly with those who are nearing death. As babies we had lullabies sung to us, so as we enter into the second birth-experience it seems fitting to offer song. I may sing a blessing (though only if I am alone with a patient!), allowing the music to form itself as I go along.

Another lovely practice is to breathe with someone who is deeply asleep or sedated. By following the breath of the person I may connect with her, and my love may be communicated at a profound level. And of course touch. Holding someone's hand in the stillness of the room can be very centring for me and helpful to them (see the section on 'Touching' in Chapter 9).

We are all different and need different things. When I die I do not want to be fussed over; but I do want to know that there are others with me as I take the next step of the journey. I think I will want their loving *presence* more than their words or touch. (I know that, if possible, I will also want the reassuring presence of my dog!)

Co-workers

A few years ago I was taking part in a spirituality workshop. The person guiding me suggested that I might visualize the passage in which Jesus and the other disciples are in a boat in the middle of a storm (Mark 4.35–41). Though this is a very familiar story to me and I was not very enthusiastic about the task, I was bowled over by what happened. I imagined myself in the boat, with Jesus asleep in the stern. I could easily sense the ferocity of the wind and the crazy movements of the boat. When we were about to sink we woke Jesus up and he and I stood up in the boat, his arm around my shoulders, and together we commanded the sea and the wind to be still. Part of me wondered if I had got carried away in my imaginings and that this was a little blasphemous, but my emergent self heard a call to be a co-worker with God.

This is a good place to be. I am standing in the midspace between two things: on the one hand, I try to do it all myself – ego-driven, my work revolving around my own achievements; on the other hand, I want to let God do it all while I feel totally useless as I wander up and down the sidelines of life's sports ground. The new place is different from both of these. I experienced the call to be a co-worker as a vote of confidence in me, and found a huge amount of energy in this visualization. I need God's arm round my shoulders but he needs my energy and love.

I will sometimes ask Jesus to come with me into the ordinary day and into demanding situations. He and I can face the lions together. My head tells me this is childish and that he is there already before I ask. But my heart says that the act of asking him to accompany me is of supreme importance:

B   If I lend you a bike, will you come in with me today to the hospice?

J   That would be great. We could have an adventure!

B   Yes ... but I'm tired. Let's not be too adventurous.

J   OK, a small adventure, a little explosion of life!

B   I don't like the word 'explosion', Jesus. Couldn't you just sit somewhere quietly, and every now and then I'll come and talk to you?

J   That doesn't sound much of an adventure ...

B   OK. Come along and we'll just see what happens shall we?

J   Fantastic! Let's make it up as we go along!

B   Jesus, could you be a little less enthusiastic do you think?

J   Umm ...

B   I need a quiet day.

J   A quiet day ...?

B   And I don't need you practising your communication skills on me.

Playfulness again

I once imagined a conversation between Jesus and myself, and when we had finished speaking I invited him to come out sailing on the sea with me. He was very excited and at one point was deliberately trying to capsize the dinghy. My sensible adult had to work hard to keep him under control, but we had great fun. Doubtless I have invented this playful Jesus as a response to the rather fear-driven, guilt-inducing pictures of Jesus I received as a child. But as other people have recognized, the words play and pray are remarkably similar. Creativity may spring from suffering but if it does not kiss playfulness on the way up it will be a dull thing indeed.

Play is so important in our work. Often I am looking ahead to the next bit of holiday, and this can keep me going. But why can't I occasionally have a holiday at work? For me the best holidays are when I slow down, notice my surroundings and am in touch with my playfulness again. So far I have only managed half a day of holiday at work, but it was a really good half day. I deliberately slowed everything down, cycled to work by a different route and became aware of birdsong, wind, chimneys, sky . . . At work I walked around slowly, waiting for people to come to me rather than rushing to find them; taking time for stillness and reflection. It was truly lovely.

When I was a chaplain at Rampton Hospital our office was situated next to the patients' library. In order to access the toilet we needed to go through the library office. We had an excellent rapport with the library staff. One week there was a discussion about toilet seats. There were far more women using the toilet than men, but for some inexplicable reason the toilet seat was often left in the 'up' position, hence the women were complaining. After many conversations on this topic I went into the toilet and put the loo brush on the rim of the toilet so that it was holding up the seat at an angle. Now it was neither up nor down.

This sort of playfulness among staff, which does not harm or put down another person, is important, especially in such environments as psychiatric institutions or hospices that act as containers for deep human experience. When we are at play we do not take ourselves so seriously. The 'place just right' is not a heavy, overserious place. A sorrowing family surrounding the bed of an elderly lady who is clearly dying can still joke about the grandson who has allegedly been following the patients' drinks trolley around the hospice corridors waiting to see if he can filch a beer. There may be lightness and even joy in the valley of the shadow.

Simplicity

'Simple Gifts' refers to 'true simplicity'. Simplicity is not naivety, still less stupidity – it is the discovery of the single eye. Seeing well is what the reflective process is concerned about, and we are constantly wiping the mirror to see what reflections are coming back to us. As the opening line of the song suggests, simplicity and freedom are brother and sister. When our listening work is simple, focused on this particular person, listening with patience, gentleness and attention, then freedom is ours too. This is a particular, paradoxical sort of freedom that is called the freedom of service. We are not free to do anything we like for we are bound by the laws of love and respect. But we are free to see clearly, free to connect and free to live fully in the moment that is given to us. Through this freedom and simplicity the person we are listening to may grasp that they are loved.

Letting go of perfection

The 'place just right' is not the same as the idealized place of Chapter 13 ('It is as it is'). Perfectionism tries to shortcut the hard work of reflection and arrive effortlessly at 'the valley of love and delight'. This is just not possible. We will only ever be good-enough carers; perfectionism is profoundly unhelpful. Even when we have become well schooled in the arts of reflection we still find ourselves pushed back into 'the place all wrong', where we feel like an outsider, are trying too hard to be helpful or are just plain scared. We still carry our wound around with us and must change the bandages regularly. But soul reflection does help us. We find we are able to bear our wound in a different way. When we plunge into despondency we have imaginative strategies that help us, and we are a little more playful in our approach to the work. We sometimes taste the joy of being in balance, and when we are off-centre we sense that there is a way back. And if all else fails we can always have a dialogue with one of our many selves.

Christ of the depths, hollow me out,
Christ of the unknown paths, send me out into the
   dark,
Christ the dreamer, dream your Kingdom in me.

Appendix
Over to you

Below, linked to their respective chapters, are some soul exercises and questions for reflection that you may like to play with. Try them out without self-criticism! Be sensitive to your needs – do not force an imaginative exercise when it just does not feel right. If you find that disturbing material is emerging, talk to someone you trust about it.

1 Many selves

1 Do the banquet exercise. First write or draw different aspects of yourself. These might be your different roles in life or different parts of your personality. Do not try too hard to make them appear; just let them emerge naturally. Then imagine the different selves in the anteroom of the hall. Finally, invite them one by one into the banqueting hall itself. What do you discover?
2 The room. Follow the exercise as described in the chapter. What is the conversation like with the Christ or the wise person? Which parts of you wish to be welcomed home and which do not?
3 Who do you talk with about your inner reactions? If you do not have one already, consider whether you might find a soul companion with whom you could share what you are discovering about your different selves.

2 Imagination

1 Still yourself as much as you can and become aware of a recent experience that has produced a very strong inner reaction. Then let yourself down into your inner self. Is there an image that comes to mind that sums up the feeling or the experience? Allow the image to develop in its own way; do not force it.
2 Spend some time reflecting on any images from sacred writings that fit with your current life experience.

3 As you listen to another person, be alert for the images and symbols they use. You might ask the person to say a little more about a particular image they give you – perhaps invite them to 'play' with it.

3 Play

1 How easy is it for you to play? Have a conversation with 'play' and see where it takes you.
2 Try doing an acrostic or drawing a picture freely – just see what emerges.
3 Is your playfulness telling you something about the way you care for others?

4 Depth

1 Read the passage about the encounter between Jesus and the Samaritan woman. Imagine yourself in the place of the woman. What happens?
2 Write down a conversation between you and your 'carer self'. Ask what that self wants in a meeting with another person.
3 Write out an encounter that touched depths in yourself and the other person.
4 What helps you most to reflect upon your work? List those things that are helpful to you.

5 Sad

1 Draw your own sadness. Take a pencil in your non-dominant hand, call to mind an experience of loss and simply let the pencil go where it wants. Do not think about what you are doing – just let the picture emerge naturally.
2 Read through John 12.24 – which tells of the grain of wheat – a few times. Centre yourself and then imagine you are the grain falling to the earth – feel the separation from the ear of corn. Then imagine yourself lying in the warm earth, and finally your life producing a green shoot of new life.
3 Imagine a conversation with a doctor in which you are given the news that you will die in a few months' time. Write it out or speak to the imaginary doctor in a chair next to you.

6 Afraid

1 Imagine your own brick wall of fear. Spend some time looking at it. Take some bricks in your hands and see what is written on them.
2 Look up the account of Gethsemane in Mark 14.32–42 or some other description of fear and suffering. Engage with the passage creatively. You may want to make a picture with pastels, create a dialogue or stay with the passage imaginatively.
3 Have you learnt anything new about your particular fears?

7 Angry

1 Read the passage about the cleansing of the Temple in John 2.13–21. Imagine yourself in the scene.
2 Have a conversation with your own anger.
3 What happens when you reflect on the words, 'I am a nice person'?

8 Outside

1 Find some crayons, felt-tip pens or pastels, take a piece of paper and draw yourself listening to another person. It does not have to be beautiful – stick-people will be fine. Then think about the space between you, and just draw. It is very important not to think too much about this exercise – just let your hand guide you. Then reflect on what you have drawn.
2 Are you aware of the 'outsider' within? How do you make contact with this part of you? What everyday experiences evoke the experience of being on the outside looking in?
3 What is it like for you to be listened to by another person?
4 What images come to mind when you think about the good space you find yourself in when you are listened to well?

9 Intimate

1 Read through the account of the anointing in John 12.1–11. Imagine you are there, as one of the disciples or as an onlooker. What happens?
2 Put yourself in the place of Mary in the story and anoint Jesus' feet. What is this like? Write out a dialogue between yourself and Jesus about it.

3 Recall an incident when as a listener you have felt uncomfortable about intimacy. What does this reveal to you?

10 Tired

1 Think of your tiredness following different activities, including caring for others. Can you identify different sorts of 'feel' to the tiredness?
2 What images come to mind when you think of your tiredness? What do they reveal to you?
3 Look at the story of Jonah in the Old Testament or another text where someone sleeps. Have a conversation with the character.
4 How can you respond creatively to the tiredness you experience?

11 Recognize me

1 If you are aware of a lack of appreciation from a person in your past (or present), try writing a dialogue with them, imagining their response.
2 Look at the passage describing the encounter between Mary Magdalene and Christ in John 20. Imagine Christ saying your name. What is this like?
3 Write an appreciation of a particular piece of work you have done.

12 Fix it

1 Recall a caring situation where you wanted to 'fix' something. In imagination live it again. What do you learn?
2 Read an account of the crucifixion such as Mark 15, or another account of immense suffering. Enter into the story imaginatively. What do you find yourself thinking, feeling and doing?
3 Have a conversation with the part of yourself that can feel out of control.

13 It is as it is

1 Find a stone that is not very beautiful. Let it sit in your hand. Then say to yourself, 'Let this stone become . . .'. See where your reflection takes you.

2 Think of a time when you have felt dissatisfied. Enter more deeply into that feeling and see what images come to you. What are you discovering?

3 Read Mark 4.26–29. In your imagination, become the seed growing secretly. What is this like?

14 Grateful

1 What are you most grateful for in the day/week that has just passed? In your imagination, savour the moments that have given you the most life. What are you least grateful for? Allow love to fill the places of hurt, confusion or loss.

2 What do you give thanks for in your listening to others? Make a list.

3 Where do you feel hard done by? Have a conversation with your hard-done-by self and see what emerges.

15 The place just right

1 Think of a time when you have experienced 'the place just right' when listening to another person. Go back to that time, relishing it, giving thanks for it. Draw it, paint it, write a poem about it . . .

2 Write down some of the ways in which you communicate without words.

3 Experiment with having a holiday at work – however you define 'work'. Deliberately slow yourself down for a few hours and notice what happens.

Notes

Introduction

1 Sally and Paul Nash, *Tools for Reflective Ministry*, London: SPCK, 2009.
2 *Caring for the Spirit* is the name of a strategy document for Hospital Chaplaincy published by the South Yorkshire Workforce Development Confederation in 2003.
3 In this section I have been greatly helped by the reflections on *ghosti* in 'The Stranger Within' in *The Laughter at the Heart of Things: Selected Essays by Helen M. Luke*, New York: Parabola Books, 2001.

2 Imagination

1 See the labyrinth at <http://www.pilgrimshospice.org/139_CanterburyTherapeuticLabyrinthGarden.html>.

15 The place just right

1 Louis J. Puhl SJ (trans.), *The Spiritual Exercises of St. Ignatius: Based on Studies in the Language of the Autograph*, Chicago: Loyola University Press, 1951, Introductory observation 15.